CW00597038

the book of love and happiness

the book of love and happiness

how to find and keep love in your life

kerry howard   mavis klein   julia lampshire

illustrations by natacha ledwidge

RYLAND
PETERS
& SMALL
LONDON NEW YORK

Designers Gabriella Le Grazie and Saskia Janssen
Editors Miriam Hyslop and Sophie Bevan
Production Patricia Harrington
Art Director Gabriella Le Grazie
Publishing Director Alison Starling

Illustrations Natacha Ledwidge

Editorial Consultant Christina Rodenbeck

First published in
the United States in 2004 by
Ryland Peters & Small, Inc.
519 Broadway
5th Floor
New York NY 10012
www.rylandpeters.com

10 9 8 7 6 5 4 3 2 1

ISBN 1 84172 590 0

A C.I.P. record for this book is available from the Library of
Congress upon request.

Printed and bound in China.

contents

Introduction   6

Part One   *by Kerry Howard*

the love coach   10

step one: know yourself   14
step two: what's your love-ability?   22
step three: believe in love   32
step four: love goals   38
step five: the right chemistry   40
step six: love now   44

Part Two   *by Julia Lampshire*

communicating love   46

step one: first impressions   50
step two: being a good listener   60
step three: where are you
     coming from?   64
step four: building rapport   70
step five: communicating
     sex appeal   76
step six: getting what you want   80
step seven: communicate now   83

Part Three   *by Mavis Klein*

the astrology of love   84

step one: the signs of love   88
step two: the transits of life   116
step three: do it now   123

conclusion   124
index   126
further reading   128

introduction

*… happiness is not an ideal
of reason but of imagination.*

Immanuel Kant (1724–1804)

This is an ambitious book. There's no doubt about that.
Its purpose is to help you bring love and happiness into your

life—and keep it there. In the
21st century, it's our role to be
our own fairy godmothers and
to show ourselves how we can
transform our lives and find the
love we deserve.

You are about to embark on
a unique step-by-step program,
put together by three experts in their fields. By following this
program, you will become a wiser, more confident person.
Love, in all its many guises, is, after all, the key to happiness,
and by creating and keeping sound, healthy relationships,
we create happiness.

This is a practical book. The techniques used are tried and
tested. You may find some of it tough going, and some of it hard
to believe. But remember, the path of true love never ran smooth.

This program to love and happiness works best if you start at the beginning and work through the pages steadily. Take your time with the book. There's no point rushing through and half-doing the suggested exercises.

In part one, Kerry Howard, the love coach, will show you how to bring love into your life. There are a lot of searching questions in this section. Questions about what it is you

 really want in your life, and how you can best change your life to achieve your goals. The human mind is a complex place, and you'll be amazed at the things you will uncover—aspirations, fears, obstacles, and passions you never even knew you

had! By working through these steps, you will be able to set your eyes—and your heart—on your dreams, and can forge a steady path to attaining them.

In part two, communications expert Julia Lampshire will show you how to keep love in your life through open and honest communication. Julia confidently guides you through the hazards of flirting and first dates. Of course, communication is vital at all stages of a relationship, whether you've just met, or you've been together for years. Often couples unwittingly establish patterns of communication which may not be working for them. This can lead to frustrations—partners typically complain that they don't talk any more, have nothing to say to each other, or their partner doesn't listen to them. Julia shows how you can overcome these hurdles to rekindle the love and happiness you both deserve.

Part three, written by Mavis Klein, our favorite astrologer, shows you how to take advantage of the movement of the planets to make changes in your life. The Astrology of Love should be a treat for you to dip into as you make your way through the first two sections of the book. See it as a reward for all the hard work you put into the two earlier chapters.

Parts one and two include a lot of exercises that you will need to do with pen and paper, so we suggest that you keep a journal or notebook. As well as being a place to keep all your thoughts and feelings, a journal is the best way of keeping track of your own process of growth, as you become ready to embrace your new love life. You will be amazed at how much you've changed by the end of this book.

All that is required of you is some time, some commitment, and a willingness to learn and change. So, sit down quietly with a notebook and pen, and begin your new life—a life filled with love and happiness! Enjoy!

the
love coach

> Who travels for love finds a thousand
> miles not longer than one.
>
> *Japanese Proverb*

For most of us, the key to happiness is
finding and maintaining real love. And for
many of us, that's easier said than done.
That's why it pays to be your own love coach.

In this chapter, you will learn how to apply life-coaching
techniques to your love life and so, take some dramatic
steps towards maximizing your potential to find, keep, and
cherish your love partner. This is a six-step program,
through which you will explore the attitudes and beliefs
you have about yourself and your past relationships, and
the impact they have had, to date, in your life. You will learn
how to deal with your emotions, and gain the courage
to make the right decisions for yourself. Using simple,
effective ways of changing old patterns of behavior
and thinking, you will explore new ways of bringing the
right relationship into your life, and will know when to
move away from the wrong one. As a result, you will take
control. From now on, you run your life and can produce
the result you want.

To be your own love coach, all you need is a notebook
to use as your love journal, a pen, and a commitment to
yourself to do these exercises, spending the time it takes
to do them well. Make sure you write down all your
responses in your journal because you will want to refer
back to them later. Be honest with yourself when you are
answering the questions because they are for you, and,
ultimately, for the benefit of your love life.

Have the courage and commitment to take action
and follow through with the exercises in this book,
and manifest them in your life.

Remember, you are responsible for your life. With these tools
to assist you, you can create the love life you really want.

know yourself

You may believe you know yourself very well. However, it's amazing how little time we spend thinking about our own needs and wants. To be able to give and receive love, you first need to know who you are.

You'll probably be surprised by how challenging many of the questions in this section are, and will discover some very interesting things about yourself. You will learn whether you have balance in your life, and where any current imbalances can be improved. You will assess your values, your strengths, weaknesses, and achievements, and you will discover any mixed messages that may be holding you back. A little soul-searching will be called for, but without developing your self-knowledge, how can you hope to attract, or even recognize, the right partner for you?

the wheel of life

While the focus of this book is love, it is important to realize that there may be other areas of your life in need of attention. By addressing these areas, you can bring your life—including your love life—into harmony.

The wheel of life is a great way to assess your current life balance. Draw up a wheel like the one shown below. The eight sections represent the different aspects of your life. See the center of the wheel as zero and the outer edge as ten. This is your score scale. Now, mark in your score of satisfaction within each area by drawing a line across the section and giving it a score—the larger the segment you create, the higher your satisfaction in that area. Move on to the next area until you have completed the wheel. You will now have a new perimeter to the circle, which represents your wheel of life.

Now you can assess your wheel—does it look round or is it a bit bumpy? If you score nine in your career and two in your health, perhaps you should consider spending less time at work and more time in the gym. Ask yourself the questions below.

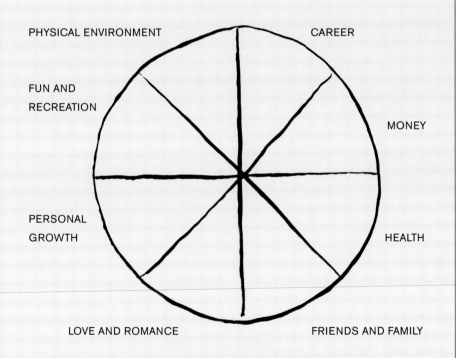

PHYSICAL ENVIRONMENT · CAREER · FUN AND RECREATION · MONEY · PERSONAL GROWTH · HEALTH · LOVE AND ROMANCE · FRIENDS AND FAMILY

Mark your scores on your wheel to create a new "wheel within a wheel." If it was a real wheel, how bumpy would the ride be?

what's in your wheel?

★ What did you notice from drawing your wheel of life?
★ How fulfilled is your life right now?
★ Where are you in balance?
★ Where are you out of balance?
★ What do you want to change?
★ How do you prioritize these sections?
★ What could you change to have the most impact on your life?
★ What would constitute a 10/10 score in each area?
★ Which areas of your life need immediate attention?
★ How would your life be different if you were to make these changes?

your values

Your values help you make choices about what you commit to in your life, which includes the kind of relationships you have and the kind of love life you enjoy. They are the qualities that define you and are at the core of who you are. How clear are you about your own value system? What is important to you? And what do you value in a relationship?

Use the questions on this page as prompts, and make a list in your journal of what you value most, both in your life and in a relationship. Your values may be one word, like "fun" or "commitment," or more specific ideas, such as "spending time in my garden," "enjoying vacations with loved ones." Jot them all down and see what you think about them. Give each value a score out of ten for its importance to you.

Now look at your three top values and check them against your life wheel. If your top value is "traveling and exploring new places," how would you hope to see this reflected in your wheel of life? Perhaps your "fun and recreation" area needs more attention to ensure you are prioritizing your top value. Your wheel may show that you are currently pursuing a goal or goals that you might not find ultimately fulfilling, since they do not incorporate the things that are most important to you. Ask yourself this question: what do I need to reassess today?

what matters to you?

★ What is important to you?
★ What do you care about?
★ What do you want in your life?
★ What do you love?
★ What makes you shine?
★ When has your life been rich and full?
★ What was important about that experience?
★ What makes you angry or frustrated?
★ What are you passionate about?

Think of a quality that is so *you* that you take it for granted and haven't written it down yet. You may like to show your list to a friend to see if they can spot anything you've missed out.

strengths and weaknesses

All of us have characteristics and abilities that make us uniquely loveable. Once again, take your journal and follow the suggestions below to help you accept your own strengths and weaknesses, and enable you to turn negatives into positives.

Acknowledging your skills and achievements will serve to remind you how far you have come, and will boost your confidence and self-esteem. Reminding yourself of challenges and obstacles you have overcome, and still face, serves to keep you positively focused.

skills and strengths

Write down all the love skills and strengths that you have—whether it's being a good listener, a loyal lover, or having a great smile. What are you really good at? Think of things that friends and partners have complimented you on, or occasions when they have turned to you for help.

learning in progress

Write down a list of what you perceive to be your weaknesses. Now take each of these and turn it into "learning in progress." So, if you have written "I am not very considerate," it becomes "I am learning to become more considerate." If you find a particular aspect on your learning list difficult, write down your concerns in your journal. They will immediately look less challenging.

collect your own fan mail

In your love journal, create a file on yourself including all your achievements. This may be things like qualifications, certificates, or promotions at work, but should also include more personal successes: friendships, party invitations, letters, cards, holiday snaps—all good-time memory stuff! Now do this visualization exercise.

Keeping the file you have made in mind, visualize your future. Remember this is your future, so make it a good one. Make it exactly as you want it—have some fun. Experience opportunities arising and new people coming into your life. See yourself receiving compliments, gifts, and invitations. This is a great time to experience what you want—and get it! Remember, you are in control so make it good!

relationship achievements

Write down a list of things that you have achieved in relationships. Include all kinds of relationships—family, work, friends and acquaintances, as well as lovers and partners. An example might be, "I established a good working relationship with my colleague X, despite the fact that he initially took against me."

are you your own worst enemy?

How do you see yourself and how do you think others see you? Do you view yourself more or less positively than other people do? List three or four positive words that you think would be used to describe you. For example:

★ A good friend

★ A supportive work colleague

★ A loving relative

This exercise is a good way to get some information about how you see yourself. If you find others are more positive about you than you are about yourself, some "learning in progress" needs to be done. Dare to love yourself as much as they do!

mixed messages

Do you dearly want to be in a loving and secure relationship, but does the idea of making that kind of commitment make you feel trapped, or worried that you may be hurt or let down?

When making decisions, we tend to think about the positive and negative aspects simultaneously, which can send your brain into overload and leave you confused. By separating and acknowledging the positive and negative aspects of a situation, you can gain a clearer insight into the various possibilities available to you. This will help you get the results you want. Write down all of the positive and negative associations you have with love and relationships. Make two separate lists, one positive, one negative. It might look something like the one below.

pros and cons of love

Positive aspects	Negative aspects
Affection	Less freedom
Companionship	Less time for myself
Security	Compromise
Reassurance	Fidelity
The status of being in a "couple"	Potential rejection and hurt
Sharing interests	Having to consider someone else's feelings
Mutual support	
Someone to talk things through with	

balance the scales

When you've completed your list, take a look at all your positive aspects—how can you maximize these in a relationship? Then look at the negative aspects—how can you minimize these? By thinking through what you want and don't want, you will be better able to select the right relationship for you.

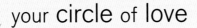

your circle of love

1   Create an imaginary space on the floor in the form of a circle.

2   Think of a situation or event in the future where you want to give and receive love, perhaps to a new partner.

3   Ask yourself what qualities you need in this situation. Think of three different qualities which would be useful (these might be, for example, trusting your partner, being sensitive to his feelings, or being able to adapt your plans to fit in around him), and think of a time when you have had those qualities—this may have occurred in a previous loving relationship, or in relationships with friends and family.

4   Now step into your circle of love and experience one of those qualities again. Make your experience as real as possible by seeing, hearing, and feeling it vividly. Then step out of your circle.

5   Repeat step 4 with each of your other two qualities.

6   Step into your circle of love again. Access all of your qualities together. See your future event with these qualities in place. Notice how it is now. Step out of your circle.

Now that you have experienced this new level of love, know that you can activate it at any time in the future whenever you need it—just by stepping into your circle!

what's your love-ability?

If you want a good relationship, you have to believe you are worthy of one. Now the love coach is going to help you really find out how loveable you feel and help you improve your feelings about yourself.

Some may believe it's egotistical or arrogant to think highly of oneself or to expect the best. In fact, there is nothing egotistical about it. Your ego is part of your self worth—the value you set on yourself.

Deep down, many people believe they have nothing to offer, and their self-esteem may have sunk to a low level. If this is true in your case, then you will put up with a lot of unacceptable behavior from yourself and others on the basis that you are not worthy of anything better. Remember, you always tend to get what you expect in life rather than what you deserve. So, if you want the very best, set high standards and have high expectations.

Now it's time to assess your own self-esteem. Answer these questions truthfully in your journal:

★ Can you take a compliment straight and say "thank you" or do you mentally deflect it, block it, or qualify it? For example, a friend tells you, "You look great tonight!" Do you:
a) Change the subject without acknowledging the compliment.
b) Think, "He's just saying that."
c) Say, "Yeah, that's because I've got half of the cosmetic counter on my face."

★ Can you list five things you like about yourself without hesitating?
Give it a try and see how you do.

★ How do you react when asked to do something new? For example, if a friend suggests you take up a new hobby together, or your boss at work asks you to take on a new responsibility, do you instantly think, "Yes, great," or is your reaction, "I'll be hopeless at it?"

★ Are you worried that one of these days you will be found out?
Can you explain this feeling? How realistic do you think your fears are?

★ What are you telling yourself when you are about to do something demanding or testing?
Do you have fears or anxieties that are holding you back from what you want?

believe in yourself

In your journal write down everything you like about yourself in the following way.

★ I like my eyes.
★ I like my smile.
★ I like my sense of fun.
★ I like my caring nature.

tackling your fears

If you discover that you are giving yourself negative messages, it is useful to take a look at what these worries are and to evaluate how realistic your fears are. You will often find that you are worrying about an improbable outcome.

be your own best friend

You can never have too many people on your side. At times in life you will encounter difficulty, unhelpful people, critical remarks, and let downs. Remember, you are the constant in your life, so be your own love coach and best friend.

Think of something that you want to do and ask yourself the following questions about it:

★ What stops me from doing …?

★ What would happen if I did …?

★ What's the worst thing that could happen?

For example, you may ask yourself, "What stops me from phoning him?" or "What would happen if I did get involved in a relationship?" If you are telling yourself "He won't want to see me again" or "I will get hurt," that little voice may well cause you some problems. Think of someone else in the same situation—how would you help them? What would you say? Now try saying these words to yourself.

your inner voice

Have you ever had one of those nagging voices in your head that just would not shut up? What are you saying to yourself about meeting your ideal partner? Too often our brains replay dialogues or thoughts over and over again. If that happens to you, try this exercise.

Turn down the volume in your head. Make the voice quieter, softer, and further away. Maybe you have one of those voices that is always limiting you. Try this. Have it say the same thing only now in a sexy or flirtatious tone. For example, "You can't do that." How does it feel now? You may even feel more motivated to do what the voice is telling you not to do!

are you positive?

Positive thinking is not about denying your feelings and emotions. Instead, it allows you to use them in a constructive way. Once you recognize negative thoughts, you can change them. This, in itself, can save you from unnecessary distress. Just as you have the ability to disturb and upset yourself, so, too, you can make yourself feel wonderful. You have the choice to live the life you want.

Every time you find yourself thinking something negative, STOP! Just be aware for a moment and ask yourself "Is this something I hear myself say a lot?" Just as negative thought is a habit, so positive thinking is, too, and you can learn to make this new way of thinking as strong a habit as your old way used to be. There are a number of tools over the next few pages to help you on your way. Try them all and record the effects they have. Emphasize the techniques that work—and don't forget to praise yourself!

ask the right questions

One way to turn negatives into positives is to ask yourself the right questions. Your brain will always try to find answers to the questions you ask it. If you ask a negative question, you will tend to come up with negative answers. For example:

★ "Why do things never work out for me?"
  "Because it never worked out before" or "Because I wasn't good enough."

If you ask positive questions, you tend to give positive answers. For example:

★ "What do I need to do to make this work?"
  "To communicate my feelings" or "To spend more time together."

pillow talk

The unconscious mind isn't able to distinguish between what is real and not real. So, if you give your unconscious mind a message, it will automatically take it as the truth. This is why affirmations are such a great way to boost your self-esteem and confidence. Even if your conscious mind doesn't accept or believe what you're saying, your unconscious will.

In your journal, write a list of affirmations. Repeating these to yourself mentally and in writing throughout the day, especially on waking and just before going to sleep, is an effective way of establishing and reinforcing these messages to yourself. Be sure to make your affirmations as positive and meaningful to you as possible. Here are some examples:

★ I, (insert your name) am loving.

★ I, … deserve love.

★ I, … am a beautiful and unique person.

★ I, … am comfortable with my body.

★ I, … am a calm and confident person.

★ I, … am fun to be with.

★ I, … am able to ask for what I want.

★ I, … am empathetic and understanding.

★ I, … am attractive.

★ I, … deserve a loving relationship.

frame your life

One of the most effective ways to affect positive change is learning how to see things in the best possible light. The meaning of all experience in life depends upon the frame you put around it. For example, a first romantic relationship ending badly could make you frame all similar experiences in the same way, telling yourself that all romantic relationships end badly.

Luckily, you have the ability to put different frames around your experiences. This process is called re-framing. The frame you put around things will inform the way you feel about the world and yourself. Changing the way you habitually see events and situations can greatly improve your love life choices and experiences.

We all know people who have become cynical after an unsuccessful relationship, whether it's friendships, family, or lovers who have left them feeling let down. They get hurt and decide to stay out of the relationship arena for good. The fact of the matter is that the relationship may, for the most part, have been great. Ignoring these good memories and focusing on the bad aspects ends up putting the worst possible frame on the experience. By changing a negative frame to see the positive aspects of the relationship, you can then move on with a positive mind-set and be empowered to create an even better relationship in the future.

the good times

The exercise of re-framing your past relationships can be simple. Rather than focusing on the negative aspects—the pain of breaking up, feelings of hurt or rejection—look instead at the reasons *why* it hurt so much to lose that relationship—it must have been pretty good. Why not literally look through some old photos and think about the good times you spent together? These are the positive feelings you can bring into a new relationship.

changing bad habits

An easy way to change unwanted behavior or an unhelpful thought process is the exercise described on these pages, called "the swish pattern." It can be used to deal with some of the most persistent problems and negative habits you may have. You can use this exercise as many times as you like on any unwanted behavior or thoughts you want to change.

1   Identify the behavior or thought you want to change. For example, perhaps you become nervous and agitated when approaching someone you find attractive. You can change this behavior to become more confident in such situations.

2   Imagine this behavior as vividly as you can. Watch yourself as if you are in a movie, picturing the scene.

3   Now make a picture of how you would like to be when you have made the desired change. For example, imagine yourself approaching someone you find attractive looking calm and confident.

4   You are now going to "swish" the two pictures so the old unresourceful behavior automatically triggers the new resourceful one. Once you connect up this triggering mechanism, anything that used to set off the old behavior will now trigger you into your new behavior. In this way, you create a whole new way to deal with what in the past may have upset you.

5   Start by imagining a big bright picture of the behavior you want to change, as described in step 2. Then, in the bottom right-hand corner of the picture, make a small dark image of the way you want to be. Take that small picture and very quickly, in less than a second, have it grow in size and brightness and literally burst through the picture of the behavior you no longer want. As you do this, say the word "woosh" in your mind. Saying "woosh" in an excited way sends powerful positive signals to your brain.

This process should only take as long as it takes to say the word. Do it now. You should be left with a big bright colorful picture of how you want to be, and the old picture has been completely destroyed.

6 Open your eyes for a moment, then close them. Do step 5 again—woosh! Now see the new picture even bigger and brighter. Pause and experience this new bright picture again.

7 Open your eyes, then close them, and do the swish pattern again five or six times. Each time, do it as fast as you can. The key to the success of this technique is speed and repetition. You must see and feel that small dark picture become huge and bright and explode through the big picture, thus replacing it with an even bigger brighter picture of how you want things to be. Now experience seeing things as you want them.

the past is part of the present

It is important to remember that most of our beliefs are generalizations based on our past experiences. Interpretations we make about what we've learned cause us to associate our beliefs with positive or negative feelings.

These generalizations guide all our actions and, in turn, the quality of our lives. Once adopted, we tend to forget that they are merely interpretations, and we begin to treat our beliefs as if they are reality, and rarely ever question them.

believe in a new you

Answer the questions in the panel (right), then, in your journal, jot down five key beliefs you hold about yourself and your relationships that may have limited you in the past. Examples could include:

★ I can't maintain a relationship.

★ I'll never meet the right person.

★ No one finds me attractive.

Now write down a list of five alternative beliefs for yourself. Ask yourself what would be a more empowering belief instead.

★ I can maintain a relationship.

★ I will meet the right person.

★ Many people find me attractive.

Visualize yourself now with your new chosen beliefs in different situations. For example, picture yourself asking someone out to lunch or suggesting you go to see a film together. Make your picture as exciting and compelling as possible by adjusting the color, tone, brightness, sounds, and volume levels.

your love beliefs

Ask yourself the following questions:

★ What is my belief about love?
★ What do I believe I deserve from being in a relationship?
★ What is my belief about having a loving and long-lasting relationship?
★ What is my belief about being able to find and attract the perfect love partner?

Now step into the picture and experience it fully. If it is exactly as you want it, great! If you'd like to make any further adjustments, go back to your picture and adjust wherever appropriate until it looks, sounds, and feels just right.

Now step into your picture again. Stand the way you stand, breathe the way you breathe, speak the way you speak, and be the way you are with your new beliefs. Pay particular attention to the way this feels in your body and notice how much more resourceful you are now.

questioning your beliefs

It is important to sit back once in a while and question your beliefs. For example, being teased at school about a certain physical characteristic may lead you to form a belief that you are unattractive, and carry this belief with you through your life, without necessarily realizing why or how it was formed. Remember, when you begin to doubt your beliefs and question their validity, you can begin to shake their very foundations so that they no longer impact on you as strongly. Start to do this by looking at your list of love beliefs and asking yourself some of the following questions:

★ How was this belief ridiculous or absurd?

★ Was the person I learned this belief from worth copying?

★ How will it ultimately affect me emotionally if I don't let go of this belief?

★ How will it affect my relationships if I continue to hold on to this belief?

If you've taken the time to really answer these questions, you may find that some of your limiting beliefs have been weakened already.

To change a belief, we must replace it with a new one. Ask yourself what the opposite is of any suspect belief. For example, if you believe that no one finds you attractive, the opposite would be that someone finds you attractive. Think of the evidence you have to back up this new belief so that you begin to feel more certain about it. As you reinforce and strengthen this belief, it will begin to direct your behavior in a new and more empowering way.

make some **changes now**

1 Write down four actions you would like to take that you have been putting off. For example, taking up an evening class or new hobby, striking up a conversation with someone you've been wanting to meet, or calling up someone you really like.

2 Under each of these actions, write down your answer to the following questions:

★ Why haven't I taken any action?

★ In the past, what negative results have I linked to taking this action?

Your answers to these questions will help you understand what has been holding you back.

3 Write down how your life will be affected if you don't change now. Even though this may feel uncomfortable, be brutally honest. The purpose is to use these feelings to move you towards taking the next and final step towards changing that behavior.

4 Write down all the positive results you will achieve by taking that new action right now. Make your list long and exciting. For example, "I will feel the pleasure of a successful date," "My self-esteem will increase and confidence grow," "I will feel strong and courageous."

step four
love goals

People who are successful in
love know what they want and
why they want it. They have
a particular mind-set for
their lives and for their
goals. These mental traits
include high motivation,
optimism, and an ability
to focus. They set
themselves high standards,
focus on the positive, and
look for multiple pathways
to success. They do not give
up—they persevere.

Prepare yourself for difficulties in relationships, but
always look for the silver lining. If you have a setback, get
back on track. Review your list of strengths, achievements,
and goals regularly. As you have completed the first three
steps in this chapter, you will now know your key love values,
abilities, and beliefs. Now, with all your love knowledge, you will
be able to clarify what you really want.

It is important that you know clearly what your goals are so that you can
move towards them. It is often easier to know what you *don't* want than
what you *do*. In this section, we'll concentrate on the positive aspects
that you are seeking from a relationship.

locating your goals

In your love journal, make a list of goals for your ideal relationship. Use this opportunity to list exactly what you want. It is not an "ought" or "should" list. Don't pay any attention to what you imagine others might think. Write down what you do want rather than what you don't. In other words, state it positively and think about what you want to bring into your life. It's usually easier to think of a problem than a goal, so you may need to work on finding your true goals. These might be, for example, "to have a stable and loving relationship while maintaining a degree of independence" or "to get married and enjoy a happy family life" or "to move in with my boyfriend."

To check that your goal is what you really want, ask yourself the questions listed below:

★ Is my goal stated in the positive?

★ How will I know when I've got it? What will it look, sound, and feel like?

★ Can I start and maintain it?

★ Where, when, and with whom do I want it?

★ What are the extra positive elements that I might gain along the way?

★ Is it worth the effort involved?

★ Is it worth the time it is going to take?

★ Am I completely comfortable with this goal?

breath of love

Now that you have your love goal, make a picture of your goal with sound and action. Pay particular attention to how it feels. Step into your picture and adjust any colors, tones, brightness, sound, and feelings to make the experience as vivid and enjoyable as possible. Step out of your picture and now, holding it in your hands, energize your image by breathing four deep breaths into it. Take your energized picture and place it in your future where you want it. Pay attention to how much more positive you feel about achieving your goal.

the right chemistry

Have you ever had one of those days when you could do no wrong, when everyone thought you were wonderful and things just fell into place? In contrast, have you ever had one of those days when you could do no right? What's the difference? After all, you are the same person, you're just in a different state of mind.

Just as there are enabling states of mind—such as confidence, love, inner strength and joy—so, too, there are immobilizing states—confusion, anxiety, depression, and fear. While the mobilizing states can tap great well-springs of personal power, the negative states only serve to leave us powerless.

altered states

As we have seen, your behavior can be a direct result of the state you are in. Therefore, you are now going to learn how to take control and access the state you want to be in at any given time. You think this sounds impossible? Well, remember a time when you were in a rage. Maybe you were arguing with your boss, ex-lover, or a friend. Remember the state you were in. Then the phone rings, and you answer in a calm and pleasant manner. Yes, you did it—you changed your state.

look at the state you're in!

As a result of external events, most people move from one state to the next without any conscious awareness or control. What creates the state you are in?

★ How you interpret what you see.
★ How you interpret what you hear.
★ Your response to the world around you.

change your tune

Our states may be altered in a variety of ways. For example, music, tastes, smells, sights, and sounds can alter your state in an instant. These stimuli can remind you of a very positive or negative time or event, which you then re-experience in your mind.

Remember a time you were feeling low, as if nothing could get you out of this state. Suddenly "that" song comes on the radio and your whole world looks and feels better. You get out of your armchair and start to dance around the room as your mood changes. Watch out for those things that put you in a positive or negative state, such as songs, poems, or places that have a special poignancy for you. Move towards the positive ones and use them to your advantage. So, if a special song makes you feel sexy and alive—play it!

model behavior

Have you noticed how some people seem to be able to talk easily to potential partners? Have you ever wondered how they do that? More importantly, have you wondered how you are going to do it?

Start by observing someone who does what you want to be able to do really well. How do they stand, move, speak, listen, make eye contact, and so on? What do you think they believe about themselves, their abilities, and attractiveness? Once you start to spot some of these key elements, you can start to incorporate them into your own behavior.

You need to say in your mind the same message as you are saying with your body. For example, if you are modeling the physical aspects of a confident person and, at the same time, telling yourself "I look stupid," you will not fully experience the benefits because you are not totally engaged with your mind and body. Try behaving "as if" (see left).

as if

What do you think the difference is between being confident and attractive and behaving "as if" you are confident and attractive? The answer is that there is no difference. If you have a tendency to "make do," or lack confidence, try this. Behave "as if" you have high expectations or "as if" you are confident. Do it for a week and notice the difference.

get physical

The way you use your body affects your emotional state. Try this exercise. Stand up and let your body slump, shoulders sag, and your head drop down. How excited, motivated, attractive, and positive do you feel? Shake your body out for a moment. Now stand tall, shoulders back, head up, eyes above eye level. Notice how this feeling compares with how you felt when you were slumped. What's the difference in your energy level, your emotional state, and your desire to go and make things happen?

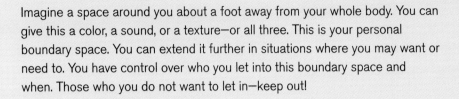

personal boundaries

Imagine a space around you about a foot away from your whole body. You can give this a color, a sound, or a texture—or all three. This is your personal boundary space. You can extend it further in situations where you may want or need to. You have control over who you let into this boundary space and when. Those who you do not want to let in—keep out!

your circle of action

1 Create an imaginary space on the floor in the form of a circle.

2 Think of a situation or event in the future where you want to take action. Perhaps this is making the first move and asking someone out.

3 Ask yourself what qualities you need in this situation. (For example, these may be self-esteem, confidence, bravery, and believing you are unique and attractive.) Think of a time when you have had these qualities, and pick the three different qualities which would be most useful.

4 Now step into your circle of action and experience one of these qualities again. Make this as real as possible by seeing, hearing, and feeling it vividly. Then step out of your circle.

5 Repeat step 4 with each of your other two qualities.

6 Step into your circle of action again. Access all of your qualities together. See your future event with these qualities in place. Notice how it is now. Step out of your circle.

Now that you have experienced this new level of taking action, know that you can activate it whenever you want to. Take this circle with you wherever you go … and take action!

love now

To find and live your ultimate love life is thought by many to be one of the greatest achievements of a lifetime.

Now that you have completed the first five steps and you know your values, strengths, and achievements, your love beliefs, goals, and how to manage your mental state, you have all the love skills and knowledge you need to achieve your heart's desire. All that remains is for you to get out there—and love!

keep on track

If sometimes things don't go according to plan, take heart. You now have all you need to get back on your feet. Reread your love journal and focus on your strengths, achievements, love-abilities, and positive beliefs. This knowledge will help you to get out of your disempowered state and take new action.

Remember you may need to reassess your love goals and your actions as you go along. Be flexible and remember that persistence pays.

write your own love story

★ In your love journal, write a sentence or a few words about your own love story so far.

★ Now write a sentence or few words about how your future love story is going to be. "From now on my love story is …."

★ Now step into your new love story. See, hear, and feel it vividly, adjusting all the sounds, feelings and colors, until it is just right. Now you are ready to live your new love life ….

communicating
love

Not the owner of many possessions will you be right
to call happy: he more rightly deserves the name of
happy who knows how to use the gods' gifts wisely …

Horace (65–8 B.C.)

How many times have you looked across
a restaurant or bar and seen a bored-
looking couple, fiddling with their drinks,
appearing to have absolutely nothing to
say to each other? And how many times have you thought,
"I don't ever want to be in a relationship like that"? Sadly, for
some, it's more like catching your reflection in a mirror,
thinking "we've become that couple—how did it ever get
to be like this?"

The key to success in any partnership is communication
and it remains a vital skill at every stage of your
relationship—whether you're just getting to know each other
or an established couple who have been together for years.

Communication begins long before you've even opened
your mouth. It's about sending out the right signals. Now
that you've worked through part one of this book, you'll have
a clear idea of what you're looking for. Now we'll ensure
that you're going the right way about achieving it.

When you first meet a new partner there is a lot to find out—interests and hobbies, personal history, hopes, fears, and dreams. For most people this will be a period of excitement as love begins to grow.

As you get to know each other, the initial excitement and high emotion begin to settle into a more stable routine. Patterns of communication become established and there is a danger that the feeling of closeness can begin to wear off.

As you read through these pages, you will learn to think about communication from different angles—from the way we use words to express our motivations to the messages we convey without even speaking a word. Whether you're looking for love or are already in an established loving partnership, you will find ideas and exercises to help you improve your communication and build happy relationships.

So—let's start communicating love!

first impressions

It is true what they say—you never get a
second chance to make a first impression,
so this section is all about making sure
you create the impact you want to make.

When you walk into a room you convey information about yourself without even opening your mouth to speak. The way you dress, wear your hair or make-up; the way you move, your bearing and posture; your facial expressions and eye contact— all these things tell others something about you.

positive impact

When asked what makes the difference between creating a good and a bad first impression, one of the main things that people say is "confidence."

A sure way to boost your confidence is to be prepared. This could mean anything from thinking through what you will wear and the impression you want to make, through to planning your opening line or topics for conversation. In this section of the book we will cover all of these issues, and there will be many hints, tips, and ideas to help you to build your own social skills and confidence.

can you be too confident?

Creating a good impression is about getting the balance right, being self-assured without being pushy, and taking part without needing to dominate or compete. It's about being relaxed and at ease with yourself and others. Being overly confident can create the impression of being arrogant, domineering, or self-obsessed. Think of a person you know who fits this description. What specifically is it that they do that crosses the boundary from self assurance to over confidence?

be prepared

Think of someone you know well that you think makes a good first impression on people. What is it about them that creates a positive impact?

Here are some examples:

★ Dressed appropriately for the situation

★ Walking and moving with purpose

★ Good posture, shoulders squared

★ Open, friendly expression

★ Good eye contact

confidence boost

As we have seen, people who make a good first impression tend to have a certain air of confidence or a presence that allows them to be their natural self with others. For those of us who are less confident, we can do things to help ourselves feel more at ease in situations we may otherwise view as stressful or uncomfortable.

It is useful to prepare in advance for an uncomfortable event that might be coming up: think what it would be like to know that you have the confidence to handle it! One way to do this is to learn from your own past experience, and the exercise on the next page teaches you how to boost your confidence by drawing on your own inner resources.

feeling confident

Think of a time when you felt confident:

★ What was the situation? Where were you? Who was there?

★ What were you doing? (For example, talking about shared experiences, just being silent together, or doing an activity.)

★ What did you see around you? (Really picture the situation—people's expressions, clothing, and your surroundings.)

★ What did you hear your friend or colleagues saying? What sounds were there other than conversation? What did you hear yourself saying? What did you think or say to yourself?

★ What sensations did you feel? How did you know you were at ease and confident? Where did you feel this in your body?

1　Think of a time in your past when you felt relaxed, at ease, and confident in a social situation. It may have been a meeting at work where you joined in the discussion, or a time when you were chatting over coffee with a friend. Try to identify a specific example and answer the questions, above, in your journal.

2　As you put yourself back into this situation you will begin to feel the sensations you felt at the time. Give these sensations and the feeling of confidence a color. Let that color to wash through your body, from top to toe. You may even like to intensify the color as you turn the feelings of confidence up a notch.

3　Add a key word or name for this feeling and associate it with the experience of the feelings and the image of the color. You may need to repeat this several times to be sure that you have recreated the feeling of confidence and can summon it when you need it.

4　Now, think of a social event when you were nervous or ill at ease. Close your eyes and take yourself to 5 minutes before you began to feel nervous.

5　Visualize the color you selected; say the key word to yourself, and build the feeling of confidence. In your mind's eye, relive the experience but with your new-found confidence. How is it different?

6　Think ahead to a social event that is coming up where you might have expected to feel slightly ill at ease. Run through a mental image of how the situation unfolds when you approach the event with confidence.

the right impression

When you meet a potential partner how can you be sure you create the impression you want to give? First you need to get clear on the message you want to convey. Do you want to appear zany and quirky? Warm and friendly? Quietly confident? Professional and remote? Fun and sexy?

Let's consider the differences between some of these styles. Be aware of the response you may get. Not everyone will warm to each of these styles and you don't want to risk turning off the very people you wish to attract as potential friends, lovers, or partners.

personality types

zany and quirky
The look:

  ★ You have individual style that stands out from the crowd. You come across as a character, perhaps witty and a bit offbeat. You may have unusual hobbies or interests.

The message:

  ★ If done without thought: "I don't care what others think." (Think of someone who looks like they've just rolled out of bed and grabbed the first thing they could find to wear.)
  ★ If done well: "I like to be different and don't mind if you are." (Think of Phoebe in *Friends*.)
  ★ If overdone: "Look at me everyone—aren't I interesting!" (Think of punk-rock extremes.)

warm and friendly
The look:

  ★ You make good eye contact, are expressive and smiling. You include others in the conversation and show interest in them, with an emphasis on *we* not *I*.

Think of a specific social situation you attended recently. For example, a work-related social function or a drink with some friends. Cast your mind back and remember your arrival at the event in as much detail as you can. Now get creative: imagine there was someone new in the group who hadn't met you before. Write down in your journal what impression she or he would have of you.

★ What message would be given from your clothing, style of dress, and accessories?

★ What would a newcomer read from your expression and gestures as you arrive? Think about the way you moved into the room and how you chose to join the group. Where did you stand or sit, and whom did you talk to?

★ How do you greet your friends and people you know? What would be different in the way you greeted this new stranger to the group?

★ Looking at the information you've gleaned from these questions, what first impression do you think you would make?

The message:

★ If too rehearsed: "I want you to like me." (Think of a slick, fawning sales person.)

★ If done well: "I'm interested to get to know you." (Think of a good host or hostess.)

★ If trying too hard: "I'm desperate for you to like me—please be my friend." (Think puppy dog.)

cool and controlled

The look:

★ You are smart; it is likely that your hair is styled and that you wear monotone outfits (usually black) with few accessories or ones that make a statement. You use minimal gesticulation, and may be slightly aloof or distant.

The message:

★ If done in a way that suggests brittleness: "Don't mess with me."

★ If done well: "I am my own person and will let you in in good time."

★ If overdone: "You're not good enough to interact with me." (Think of the supermodel stereotype.)

fun and sexy

The look:

★ Your clothing plays to a physical asset, and your make-up emphasizes lips and eyes. You choose accessories that draw attention, and your hair is often long or in a slightly unkempt style. Your body language is relaxed.

The message:

★ If done badly, overaccentuating a physical feature: "Look at my legs, but don't notice my personality."
★ If done well: "I know I look my best and I'm out to have fun."
★ If overdone: "I'm on the hunt tonight."

look in the mirror

The following exercise is designed to help you assess your "look" to ensure you get the right balance.

1 Go to your wardrobe and select an outfit that you feel most reflects your chosen style. Put on your make-up, do your hair, and select accessories as you would if you were going out socially.

2 Think of a friend or family member whose opinions you respect and who cares about you—what would they say about your chosen style?

3 Find a full-length mirror. If possible, practice walking towards the mirror to see how naturally and easily you move. Pull a chair over to the mirror and observe the way you sit and your posture. What minor changes could you make to fit better with the look that you wish to create? (Of course, if you have access to a video camera your feedback will be even better!)

be yourself

As a general rule, it's best to play to your strengths rather than pretend to be something you're not. If you are usually quiet and withdrawn, you will not become the life and soul of the party purely by dressing and behaving differently—in fact, you are more likely to make yourself feel ill at ease and self-conscious. The key is to become more comfortable and confident with an image that suits your own personality.

getting feedback

This game is a creative way to find out what others think of you. Play it with friends or family in a light-hearted and fun way.

Each person takes it in turns to ask the others in the group to answer this question: "If I were an animal, what animal would I be?"

When each individual has given their answer, ask each in turn to say why they picked the animal they did. For example: "I said John would be an elephant because he's big and strong, and he never seems to forget anything!" (Not "I picked an elephant because John has a photo of an elephant on his desk," which doesn't give any real insights.)

The game can be continued for further rounds by substituting other questions:

★ If I were a household object, what would I be?

★ If I were an item of clothing, what would I be?

★ If I were a drink, what drink would I be?

★ If I were a food, what would I be?

★ If I were a color, what would I be?

choose your words

So, you've prepared your outfit and thought about the impact you wish to make. However, it might also be useful to spend a moment or two thinking about your opening lines and how to make small talk. If you see someone you're attracted to, what will you say?

Many people find small talk uncomfortable. Typically, people will ask what you do for a living, what interests or hobbies you have, where you live or where you come from, what films, books, or music you enjoy. Think about how you usually respond to these questions and the impact your replies will make on a person you've just met.

naming game

One of the things that may concern you is how to remember others' names when first introduced. A handy tip is to silently repeat their name three times whilst shaking their hand or making eye contact. Then use their name in conversation as soon as possible to help reinforce your memory. If you do forget someone's name, don't be embarrassed to ask them again later.

chit-chat

It's useful to look more closely at the different types of answer you can give to simple questions, and to consider the impression each different type of response will make on the person you're talking to. For example, think about responses to the question "What do you do for a living?"

★ "Oh, me, I just work at … company."
★ "I work at … company, I don't know if you've heard of it? I'm in the … department and I'm responsible for …. How about you?"
Or
★ "I'm unemployed."
★ "I'm not in employment at the moment but I spend my time doing …."
Or
★ "Oh no—don't talk about work—I hate my job!"
★ "I don't enjoy my job much at the moment and I've started looking for something which involves more work with people."

The trick to small talk is keeping the conversation flowing, and the best ways to do this are:
★ To provide information that others can pick up on.
★ To ask questions of others.

Next time you go to a social event where you will meet new people, spend some time preparing your answers to standard questions like these. It may also be helpful to prepare a few topics that you can introduce into the conversation. A good starting point is to think of recent events, topical news, or new films on which others may have an opinion. Of course, having got the conversation going the most important thing is to listen ….

being a good listener

Think of your closest friend, the one you enjoy spending time with and can discuss your problems with. Chances are that this person is both a good conversationalist and also a good listener. Listening is a key skill found in happy relationships.

Listening isn't as simple as you might think. A good listener makes space for others when they need it and listens without judging, without trying to solve your problems for you, and without forcing their opinions on you. None of us is perfect and we will all display different types of listening at different times—some better, some worse. The key is to make sure that you're not stuck in one style.

recognizing different types of listening

lights are on but no one's home

You're guilty of this when you suddenly realize your friend has been telling you a story for the past five minutes but your attention has completely wandered off and you have no idea at all what she's been talking about. In short, while you've been nodding in the right places, you really haven't been listening at all. (This is a key danger in long-term relationships as we can mistakenly assume we've heard it all before.)

when's my turn?

This is when you've heard something that reminds you of a great story you want to share and you can't wait for the speaker to finish so that you can tell your story. In this instance, you've usually stopped listening as soon as you got your idea.

you're wrong or you're right!

As you listen, you are sifting the information against your own values, experiences, and beliefs to decide which bits you agree with and which you disagree with. When you listen in this way you are judging what is said. You may find that you spend a lot of time trying to convince the other person that your point of view is right.

different maps of the world

This is when you listen with an open mind. You may hear things you disagree with or that are different from your own experience but you are able to accept these differences in opinion and do not feel the need to convince the other person to agree with your own viewpoint. In successful partnerships, the individuals have recognized that they bring different things to the relationship and they respect these differences.

empathic listening

This involves listening to the underlying message as well as the words that are said. You sense the emotional content and the real needs of the other person. This is an important skill in long-term relationships. Everyone who's been in a relationship knows that an argument about putting out the trash or doing the dishes is really only the presenting issue. Underlying this there are real needs and feelings that are not being addressed. For example, a need to be recognized (not to feel taken advantage of). In any emotionally charged situation you need to develop the skill of listening beyond the words.

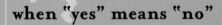

when "yes" means "no"

Think about someone you know well—maybe a close friend or family member. How do you know when she or he really means "no" even though they have said "yes"?

★ Is it their tone of voice or speed of speech?
★ Is it their facial expression?
★ Is it their body language?
★ Is it their eye movements?

If you respond to the underlying message, this is an example of empathic listening. For example, "You said yes, you would like to come to the movies with me, but it doesn't sound like you're that keen—is there something else you'd rather do?"

Think about how you might give mixed messages, saying one thing but meaning the opposite. What impact could this have in a loving relationship?

learning to listen

How can you improve your own listening?
As with all things, practice makes perfect,
so here are some tips to get you started.

1 Ask questions that explore something the speaker has just said. "You said you enjoyed your holiday in Antigua. What was it you liked about it? Do you have any photos with you?"

2 Summarize the key points made by the speaker using different words that convey the same message. "It sounds like the Caribbean is a great place to go for a week's break."

3 Build on the previous point made by the speaker. "You said you enjoyed your holiday in Antigua. I've heard that the diving is really good there."

4 Share relevant personal information. "Antigua? I've never been there—I've always wanted to go to the Caribbean but I don't fancy such a long flight."

5 Use key words or phrases to reflect back what you've heard. "It does sound exotic and relaxing the way you describe it."

6 Listen for the underlying message, read the non-verbal communication and trust your intuition. Reflect back your impressions: "You said you're looking forward to your next holiday, but you don't look that happy about it."

where are you coming from?

Different people have different styles of communication—so much so, in fact, that you may wonder if you are even speaking the same language! By understanding these differences, we can learn to communicate better with those we love.

The way in which we communicate reveals information about our personalities, interests, and preferences. The following are some common communication patterns regarding how you take in and sort information. Draw up a box in your journal, as shown on page 67, and try to classify yourself, your loved one, and someone you find it very hard to communicate with.

communication styles

overview or specific detail

★ Do you prefer to have an overview of a story and not want to know any of the details? When people tell stories with lots of detail, do you

battle of the sexes

You only have to be around the opposite sex for a short while to realize that men and women have very different ways of communicating.

Women are typically seen as:

★ Chatty and gossipy, enjoying conversation.

★ Expressive about people, emotions, and feelings.

★ Able to multi-task (therefore can watch TV and chat).

★ Talking to get the problem out in the open rather than to find a solution.

★ Able to notice and understand non-verbal communication.

★ Thinking out loud about problems or activities.

Men are typically seen as:

★ Monosyllabic and comfortable with silence.

★ Expressive about objects, things, and facts.

★ Focused on one thing at a time (therefore hate to chat while parking the car).

★ Raising problems only to explore solutions (hence assuming that if a woman raises a problem, she wants ideas on how to solve it).

★ Unaware of non-verbal communication and subtle messages.

★ Thinking silently (seeing women's "self talk" as rambling and scatty).

These are, of course, generalizations but they are often familiar enough to make us smile as we recognize ourselves and our loved ones.

find yourself trying to hurry them up to get to the main points?
Do you tell stories in overview?
Or

★ Do you like to know lots of detail—how, where, what, when, who? Do you find yourself asking lots of questions when people tell stories which lack detail? Do you tell stories with lots of detail?

visual, auditory, or sensory

★ Do you tend to describe how things look? Do you like to see the person you're talking to, preferring face-to-face conversations to speaking on the telephone? Do you use gestures or drawings to help explain yourself? Do you use words like "clear," "perspective," "focus?"

Do you use phrases like "I see what you mean;" "that looks good to me;" "It appears to me"?

Or

★ Do you notice accents and find it easy to recognize voices? Do you pick up on people's tone of voice? Are you likely to look away from a person when listening to them? Are you more at ease talking on the telephone than face to face? Do you use words and phrases like "it sounds as if we're in tune;" "that rings a bell;" "I heard alarm bells when he ...;" "on the same wave length"?

Or

★ Do you focus on the feelings behind the words? Do you like to touch, and be hands-on, rather than to observe or listen passively? Could you imagine yourself using words and phrases like "feel," "warm," "cool;" "I grasped the point he was making;" "... in touch with ...;" "let's not leap to conclusions;" "we need to find a balance;" "I feel it in my bones"?

toward or away

Think of something you want. ("I want to meet a man and fall in love").

Now ask yourself why you want it.

★ Do you use language that implies moving towards what you want? ("... because I want to have someone to share adventures with ....") Do you use words like "get," "achieve," "benefits," "have," "attain"?

Or

★ Do you use language that implies moving away from what you don't want? ("... because I don't want to be lonely when I'm old.") Do you use words and phrases like "avoid," "problems," "resolve," "sort out," "mistakes," "get rid of."

structure or options

Think of the way you approach tasks.

★ Do you like to know the best way to get something done? Do you like to have a structure or process to follow? In conversation, do you explain things sequentially, telling stories step by step? If interrupted, do you return to the beginning? Do you use words and phrases like "method," "system," "routine," "the best way," "tried and tested"?

Or

★ Do you like to have options and choices in getting things done? Do you like to decide as you go along? Do you like to keep your options open? In conversation, will you happily flit from one topic to another? Do you use words or phrases like "options," "choice," "flexibility," "adapt," "bend the rules"?

similarity or difference

Think about two people that you know.

★ When you start to compare them, do you start by noticing ways in which they are the same? In conversation, do you tend to look for things that you agree with in what the speaker has to say? Do you tend to take in information by finding points of commonality with what you already know and understand?
Or

★ When you start to compare them do you notice ways in which they are different? In conversation, do you tend to look for things you disagree with in what's been said? Do you take in information by challenging it and finding points that are different to your own beliefs and understanding?

communication preferences

As you read through the communication styles, try to classify yourself, a loved one, and someone you find it hard to get on with. By referring to this table, next time you want to communicate something important to someone, think about ways in which you could change your style of communication to help him or her find it easier to understand.

	Me	My boyfriend	Someone I don't get on with so well
Overview/specific detail	....	....	....
Visual/auditory/sensory	....	....	....
Toward/away	....	....	....
Structure/options	....	....	....
Similarity/difference	....	....	....

working with different communication styles

It's key to note that there are no rights and wrongs in any of these communication styles. They merely reflect differences in preference. Recognition of these preferences can be helpful in a number of ways.

1 It can help you to acknowledge that there's more than one way of experiencing the world and your way isn't the only way!

2 You can identify your own preferences and notice the effect your communication style has on others. If it is not having the effect you want, it may be possible to modify aspects of your style—if in doubt, ask for feedback from friends and co-workers. (It's probably safest to experiment with different approaches amongst your friends first!)

3 You can notice others' communication styles and from this, identify their different preferences and ways of behaving. This helps you to accept approaches that may be very different from your own. For example, if you recognize that your boyfriend always disagrees with you at first before coming around to your way of thinking, this could just be because this is the way he takes in information—looking for points of difference in order to understand. By understanding this, you're less likely to take offence and feel criticized.

4 You can find better ways to communicate with people you care about. For example, if you've noticed that your lover is very visual, you can help him to understand your points by painting a verbal picture, telling him what it looks like to you, and providing illustrations.

5 Next time you have a miscommunication or an argument, think about whether you are disagreeing about content or whether you are, in fact, both saying the same thing but in different words!

communication case study

Imagine a loving relationship where the woman is interested in specific detail, moves away from problems, and looks for structure. The man has a preference for overview, moves toward what he wants, and looks for options. They've agreed to buy a boat and go sailing around the world. She talks about how they can get away from their problems; he talks about the places he wants to visit. She wants to investigate different types of boat, and has worked out a process to sort through the information and ensure they get the best one. Meanwhile, he's not interested in the details but has pulled out a map and identified different routes they could take.

If they understand their different styles of thinking and communicating, the two approaches will be complementary. If they get frustrated by their differences, they may decide to abandon their shared dream and go their separate ways!

building rapport

Have you ever noticed that when two people are getting on well, they will often be sitting in the same position and seem to be moving in harmony with one another? One may almost act like a mirror image of the other.

This is sometimes referred to as the dance of rapport—as one person reaches for their drink, so does the other; as one leans back, so does the other. When we are getting on with someone and in harmony, we often naturally match their movements without even being aware of it.

Similarly, if two people aren't getting on and have lost rapport, they will often sit and move in completely different ways. Their postures, gestures, and expressions may all be at odds. (Next time you're in a social setting or a meeting, make a point of looking out for these natural phenomena of matching and mismatching.)

What do we mean by the term rapport? Rapport means a relationship of harmony or affinity. When people are in rapport they have established some common ground and mutual understanding. It does not mean they necessarily agree 100 percent—it doesn't even mean they have to agree at all! It does, however, suggest they have an empathy and can hear, recognize, and appreciate each other's point of view.

matching others

Most of the time we create rapport with others easily, naturally, and at an unconscious level. Sometimes, however, it may help to know how to establish rapport by consciously making an effort to match others.

There are four main ways to match others, which are listed overleaf. (All should be used discreetly and with care to ensure you don't appear to be making fun of the other person.) At a more general level, you can also match style of dress and presentation. For example, when going for a job interview, when a smart appearance is expected, you would usually dress appropriately and not turn up in jeans and a t-shirt. If you have ever turned up to a social event wearing inappropriate clothing, you probably recall how awkward you felt being under- or over-dressed for the occasion.

ways of talking

Notice and match the following:

★ Speed of speech

★ Volume

★ Voice tone and pitch

For example, if you are talking with someone who is quietly spoken and takes pauses between their utterances, it will create rapport if you match them rather than gabble on, fast and furiously!

body posture

Look out for the following:

★ Muscle tone—tense or relaxed?

★ Symmetry—are they aligned and symmetrical or asymmetrical?

★ Flow—are they controlled and precise? Free flowing and graceful? Staccato?

Matching posture can be easily overdone, so be careful not to be too obvious as the person may think you are making fun of them. Assume a similar posture and position. Match their movement discreetly as they change posture.

rhythms of movement

Notice and match the speed and rhythms of the other person when they are talking, and use the same when you speak. For example, if the person illustrates points with their hands, you do the same when you speak. If they are jiggling their foot or moving their head a lot, you may choose to match the rhythm (but not the specific action) by drumming your fingers or moving a pen at the same tempo.

facial expressions and movements

Notice and match the following:

★ Frequency of smiles

★ Movements of eyebrows—raising or frowning

★ Head nods

For example, if the person has a serious expression, nodding occasionally but rarely smiling or using facial expressions, it will create rapport if you match them rather than grinning broadly, using animated expressions, and nodding vigorously!

experiment with matching

Before you go out to use your new-found observations and skills in the real world, make time to practice with a friend. Try the following exercises to experience the impact of matching or mismatching rapport.

1 Sit and chat with your friend about a topic which you both agree on. Match him or her using the techniques listed opposite.

2 As the conversation continues, deliberately begin to mismatch.
   ★ Change your posture.
   ★ Speak faster or slower, louder or softer than them.
   ★ Use different facial expressions.
   ★ Move at a different speed and rhythm.

3 Notice how it feels for you at step 1 and 2 above. Ask your friend to comment on how it felt for them and how easy it was to keep the conversation going. Ask him or her to tell you how to improve your matching to make it subtle and effective.

Repeat this exercise, but this time discuss a topic where you disagree or have different opinions. Notice how maintaining rapport, by matching, changes the nature of the conversation and the emotional reactions, despite disagreement.

breaking rapport

Just as we naturally use matching to create rapport, we also use mismatching to break dialogue or rapport. This behavior, often unconscious, signals to the other person that the conversation is over.

Think about how you politely signal that you want to end a conversation.

★ You look away.

★ You change posture. For example, you turn your body slightly away if standing, or if sitting, you move toward the edge of your seat getting ready to stand.

★ You change the speed or pitch of your voice.

We also use mismatching when we wish to signal that we don't want to talk with someone—the social bore chatting you up in the nightclub; your friend who keeps interrupting your favorite TV program; your mother who you want to get off the phone. However, not everyone has the social skills to read these subtle messages, and you may well have had the experience of someone who doesn't seem to recognize these signals and keeps the conversation going despite your strong non-verbal hints! In these cases, we often have to "turn the volume up" and express the message in words.

mismatching

Mismatching is also used to convey other social messages. For example, if a person remains standing whilst talking to someone who is seated, this may be a means of signaling authority or hierarchy. In meetings, an individual who wants to maintain control of the group will frequently stand to present their ideas (mismatching the group). When the discussion is thrown open to all, he or she will sit down amongst the group, signaling they are one of them.

step five
communicating sex appeal

Many people believe that sex appeal depends on having the perfect figure. Too often we waste time and energy dieting or squeezing into clothes which are uncomfortable and too tight. In reality, sex appeal is much more than looks.

Have you ever noticed how a fairly plain woman can convey masses of sex appeal or how a very beautiful woman can have none? Similarly, think of one of the many male film stars with perfectly average looks but who still seems to exude sex appeal. This is because sexiness is about more than just appearance. It is an attitude, a state of mind, a self belief.

So, how do you create your own sex appeal? It helps to get into the mind of the opposite sex and find out what appeals to them.

If you have a circle of male friends, do some asking around: ask about women they find sexy and ask specifically why. Also ask about the sorts of things which they find a turn off. Repeat the exercise with a circle of female friends, asking them what they find sexy in men. What are the key differences?

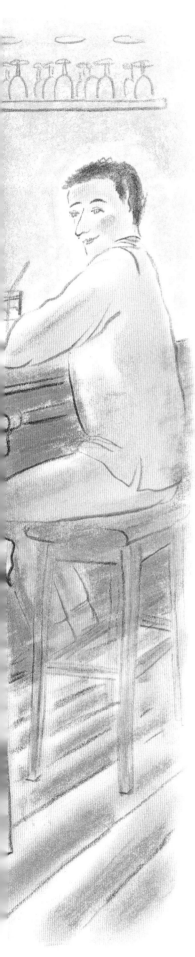

what men find sexy

flirtatiousness

A flirt plays up to the male ego. The man is flattered by the attention and, in turn, feels sexy. If you want to make this your own style of sex appeal, watch and learn from other flirts. Some general tips: Make brief eye contact across the room, look away, and look back three times to show interest. When in conversation, look deep into his eyes. Hold eye contact slightly longer than usual. Listen attentively, head on one side, exposing your bare neck. Moisten your lips with your tongue, play seductively with your hair, or with your drink. Accidentally press against him or brush his hand with yours.

sensuality

A sensual woman is in touch with her senses and relishes having beautiful things around her. A sensual woman lives predominantly in her body rather than her mind. Typically she will move in a relaxed, flowing, graceful way without self-consciousness. If this sounds like your type of sex appeal, you should indulge your senses—wear clothing which has texture and sensual shape; use perfume and body scent; take pleasure in your food and drink; create a sensuous ambience in your home.

intelligence and capability

This is a woman who has confidence in her ability. She may be a successful career woman, a great mom or someone who is an expert at a hobby or with a keen interest. The key is that she knows she is good at what she does and this confidence comes across. If this sounds like you, find ways to play to your strengths. Let your passion shine through in your conversation.

playfulness and sense of adventure

This can be a slightly quirky form of sex appeal. It might be shown in playful physical behavior one to one—romping on the floor, chasing each other down the street—or a sense of adventurousness. It might also be demonstrated through a sense of fun and spontaneity in suggesting activities. This is the kind of woman who is fun to be around and makes any activity an experience to enjoy and remember.

being enigmatic

Men are conditioned to enjoy the "chase" and they find a woman that they can't quite work out, somehow elusive and attractive. If you are an open book, this is not for you. However, if you want to create an air of mystery, don't reveal too much about yourself initially.

a specific physical attribute

This may be a nice figure, a beautiful face, a shining head of hair, an accent, or tone of voice. If you know you have a particular asset which people find sexy, then play up to it and make the most of it.

what women find sexy

While many of the above hold true for women, there are a few additional keys to sex appeal which women will look for in men.

power

This may be related to finance, type of job, or status. Often they are evident as the visible trappings of wealth and status. For some, the red Porsche does the trick, for others, it's the position on the board of directors.

humor

When a man makes a woman genuinely laugh, it is very sexy. It's unlikely that you'll tire of someone who can still make you laugh.

attentiveness

If a man listens and pays attention to his partner, often she will be hooked.

romance

This isn't just the traditional flowers, wine, and candle-lit meals, but the small gestures that show he's thinking of you. Women love to be shown that they are loved.

what do you find sexy?

Think about your own previous partners or people that you've found attractive in the past. What was it that attracted you to them? What is it you found sexy as you got to know them? List as many attributes as you can think of in your journal, adding your own ideas.

★ Their eyes? "He has such deep brown eyes;" "His eyelashes are amazing."

★ Their smile? "I love the way his eyes twinkle when he smiles;" "he's got such a gorgeous grin."

★ Their figure? "He's got such a cuddly body;" "He looks great in everything he wears."

★ Their voice? "He's got such a sweet accent;" "His voice is so deep."

★ Some specific aspect of their body? "I just love his broad hands;" "His arms are great."

★ Their hair? "He always looks well groomed;" "I love his curls."

★ Their looks generally? "He looks so French!" "He has such style."

★ Their sense of humor? "He just makes me laugh."

★ Their conversation? "We can talk for hours."

★ Their skills and abilities? "I always admired people who were good at creating things."

★ Their personality? "He is so different from me, we really complement each other;" "We love doing the same things."

★ Their job or position? "He has such a powerful job—he makes such important decisions."

★ The fact they remind you of someone else you admire? "He is so much like my brother."

Ask your friends about what they find sexy. Chances are you will find a number of differences in your lists.

say what you want

If we can learn to express our views and feelings openly, honestly, and appropriately, we are more likely to build happy and successful loving relationships.

Even when you love someone, there are times when you need to assert yourself and make your own needs explicit. This is true of any relationship. Whether your relationship is in its early days or you've been together for years, there will be times when you notice that you don't feel happy or comfortable about something, no matter how petty it may seem:

★ I don't know why I always end up driving!

★ He never does the dishes!

★ Why do we always end up going out with her friends?

★ We never go to see the films I like!

Sometimes we all fall into the trap of expecting others to guess what we want or need. "If he loved me he'd know that I want X." "If she really knew me she'd just know I don't want Y." Not only is this unfair and unreasonable, it's also a sure-fire way to be disappointed. We're making others accountable for our own happiness, then sitting back and waiting expectantly. Assertive communication is about taking ownership of your thoughts, feelings, and needs, and expressing them in a way that is clear, honest, *and* respectful. It's not about getting angry; it's not about who is in the right and who is in the wrong; and it's not about blame.

removing blame and expressing needs

Here's a simple recipe you can use to help you make your thoughts, feelings, and needs clear to someone without blaming or taking the moral high ground. Next time you get upset, angry, or sad about something your loved one has done (or not done), stop and review the following steps.

1   Describe the situation objectively to yourself. What really happened? What would an observer have seen and heard? Try to focus on the facts.

2   What am I thinking about what happened? What am I telling myself about the situation? This is usually some kind of judgement like "it's unfair" or "he shouldn't do that."

3   What do I feel as a consequence of what I'm thinking at step 2? This should be an emotion—sad, jealous, left out, disappointed ….

4   What do I usually do as a consequence of what I feel at step 3? This is often negative and destructive behavior—shouting, sulking, storming out ….

5   Go back to step 3 and the emotion that is underlying your negative thoughts and behavior. Listen to that emotion and ask yourself: what is it I really need? "I need a hug;" "I want to feel loved and cared for;" "I want to be invited too."

6   Pull all this together into an open and honest communication that ends with a request relating to what you want or need.
For example:
"When you did/said/didn't do A, I thought/think B. When I think that I feel C, because I want/need D. So would you consider E."

on the receiving end

If you are listening to someone else expressing themselves in a way that suggests strong emotions, it is important that you show empathic listening (as we explored earlier, see page 62) and make a point of listening beyond the words. Ask yourself, "what is the emotion she or he is expressing? What do they really need right now?"

By combining clear expression of your needs with great empathic listening, you have a winning formula for loving communication! And loving communication leads to loving long-term relationships.

ways to say "I love you"

Some people express their love readily and frequently through words. For others, the words "I love you" don't come easily—but this doesn't always mean to say the emotions aren't there. Some prefer to show their love in other ways. It may be jetting you off for a surprise weekend in Paris or making you breakfast in bed, writing poems or buying flowers—there are many different ways to say "I love you."

★ Take a moment to think about the different ways in which you show you love and care for someone.
★ What's the most romantic and loving gesture you have ever made for someone you loved?
★ Think about how you like others to show their love for you.
★ What's the most romantic and loving gesture you can recall that someone has made for you?

step seven

communicate now

We've explored communication in the context of finding and building loving relationships from a number of angles. Now's the time to put this into action! How are you going to apply your learning?

Over the course of this chapter, you should have noticed aspects of your behavior that were positive, and others that need to be improved on. Make a note in your journal of the behavior you want to start, what you want to stop, and what you think you're doing right.

To help me find the love and happiness I deserve in my relationship(s), I will …

Start
....
....
....
....

Stop
....
....
....

Continue
....
....
....
....

Good luck!

the astrology
of love

> We are never so happy nor so unhappy
> as we imagine.
>
> *Duc de la Rochefoucauld (1613–1680)*

How useful can astrology really be? After all, you probably know plenty of happy couples in supposedly "incompatible" signs. And a few unhappy ones who should be ideally suited. This chapter isn't about who you should or shouldn't fall in love with. Rather, it is, much like the rest of this book, about self-knowledge, which is the key to happiness. If you can recognize the weaknesses and strengths in yourself and your relationship, you've crossed the biggest hurdle to finding and keeping love.

The first step in the Astrology of Love is to investigate your Sun sign. Don't use your character outline given in these pages as an excuse to fall into the same old bad habits. Use it as a mirror, and ask yourself this question: "Am I being the best that I can be?" Then look up how you get along with other signs. Some relationships may be easier, but often it's the tough ones that are the most rewarding.

The next step is to explore the transits of your life.
Throughout our lives, our pleasures, preoccupations, and
challenges are determined by both our unique individuality
and the stage of life that we share with all others of
approximately the same age as ourselves. In childhood and
adolescence, our stage of development tends to be more
influential than our individuality; in adult life, our individuality
can become more influential. Nevertheless, there are clearly
defined stages in adult life that we all experience.

All of us sail through life's choppy waters guided by the
movement of the planets. Being prepared for the next leg
of the journey can only make it easier to
navigate. So, figure out
where you are on life's
journey, where you are
going, and how it
can help you
maximize your
happiness.

step one

the signs of love

Whereas looking at your Sun sign alone cannot give you a detailed description of your characteristics in the way that a horoscope based on your precise time and place of birth can, it is very valuable in its own way. Your Sun sign describes the core of your nature, which you share with all other people of that Sun sign, however different or similar you may seem in other ways.

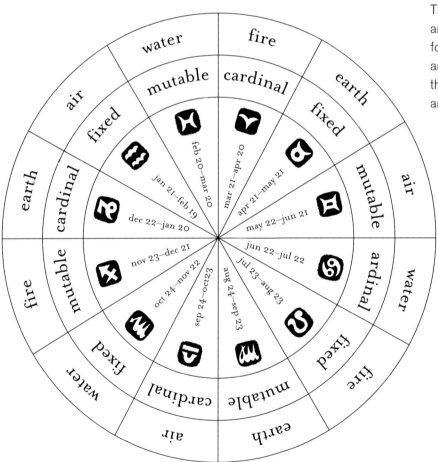

The twelve signs of the zodiac are distributed amongst the four elements—Fire, Earth, Air, and Water—and amongst the three modalities—cardinal, fixed, and mutable.

Find out your own and your partner's Sun signs for quick insight into personality. But don't get too hung up on a few simple adjectives—people are complex creatures. Sun-sign astrology should always be treated for what it is—a very broad overview of character. It's up to you to fill in the detail. Nevertheless, pay close attention to your obstacles and challenges. You may well gain some insight into what holds you back in life and love.

the elements & the modalities

Fire
+ Fire is courageous, self-assertive, idealistic and visionary, stimulating of creative expression, active, ardent, and strong.
– Fire is ruthless and self-imposing, fanatical, destroying the efforts of others, wasting energy through excess, self-indulgent, and loud.

Earth
+ Earth is a good provider, has a good sense of time, is deeply understanding, and utterly reliable.
– Earth is stingy and hoarding, lacks emotional awareness, is ultra-conservative and coarse.

Air
+ Air is sociable, inventive, intelligent, alert, objective, and full of ideas.
– Air is superficial, garrulous, repetitious, hyperactive, nervous, aloof, and cold.

Water
+ Water is compassionate, understanding, artistic, romantic, and sensitively reserved.
– Water is paranoid and hysterical, lives in a fantasy world, manipulatively controls others, and exaggerates feelings histrionically.

Cardinality
+ Cardinality is enterprising, forceful and assertive, creative and independent.
– Cardinality is bossy, ruthlessly self-seeking, impatient, and opportunistic.

Fixity
+ Fixity is loyal, purposeful, reliable, and conservative of values and resources.
– Fixity is opinionated, inflexible, stuffy, stubborn, and habit-bound.

Mutability
+ Mutability is cooperative, compromising, flexible, and appreciative of all points of view.
– Mutability is nervous, restless, lacking in conviction, and uncommitted.

how to use your sun sign

Our various talents and challenges are the two sides of the one coin, and are an essential part of each and every one of us.

See how you can apply your special qualities to your love life. Think about how using your talents could make you happier. Often, people find that they may not manifest the character traits of their sign in an overt way. The Sun sign is somehow hidden. If this is the case with you, think about bringing your Sun to the fore of your personality—after all, that is the essential you, and living your Sun to the full is more likely to make you happy.

Learning to meet your challenges head-on can make you feel stronger and more secure. Take each one of your obstacles and challenges in turn, and try thinking carefully about one a week for the next few weeks. For example, if you are a Pisces, ask yourself: "Am I too self-effacing? Do I have trouble claiming credit for my achievements?" Answer honestly. If you find it's an area you could improve on, set yourself some challenges—learn to sing your own praises! Once you feel satisfied that you're doing okay in that area, move on to the next suggestion until you have fairly answered each challenge.

make the most of your sign

★ Look (unflinchingly!) at your obstacles and challenges, talents and gifts.
★ Be glad of your talents and gifts but not scornful of other signs who lack them.
★ Accept your obstacles and challenges without envying other signs who lack them.

compatibility

People often talk metaphorically about the "chemistry" between two people but, astrologically, this is literally the case. The wonderful (and sometimes terrible) truth is that when we interact with other people, our horoscopes become unavoidably entangled.

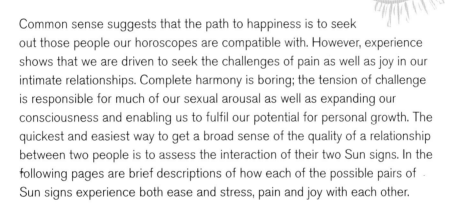

Common sense suggests that the path to happiness is to seek out those people our horoscopes are compatible with. However, experience shows that we are driven to seek the challenges of pain as well as joy in our intimate relationships. Complete harmony is boring; the tension of challenge is responsible for much of our sexual arousal as well as expanding our consciousness and enabling us to fulfil our potential for personal growth. The quickest and easiest way to get a broad sense of the quality of a relationship between two people is to assess the interaction of their two Sun signs. In the following pages are brief descriptions of how each of the possible pairs of Sun signs experience both ease and stress, pain and joy with each other.

how to use your sun sign compatibility

If you are in a relationship, putting aside all sense of self-righteousness, and without seeking to praise or blame yourself or your partner, think carefully about the tensions that exist between you. In what ways have each of you grown through the challenges of the relationship? Your partner's perception may be different from yours, so ask for his point of view and reciprocate with yours. You may both be surprised!

If you aren't in a relationship, talk to a close friend about the tensions that have arisen between you and how you have grown closer through those challenges. Also think about past relationships and the tensions that existed in them. What did you learn from them? Did those clashes put the spark into your relationship?

ARIES

cardinal, fire

march 21–april 20

Talents and gifts
Honesty, enthusiasm, efficiency, leadership.

Obstacles and challenges
Aggressiveness, impatience, scorn of others' weaknesses, selfishness.

You are imaginative and alert, energetic and restless. Nobody can accuse you of laziness or procrastination—you are a get-up-and-go adventurer.

You are decisive and punctual and expect the same of others. You are a born entrepreneur, but impatient with everyday tasks that are repetitive and are intolerant of people whose style is gentler or more cautious than your own.

You are ardent, enthusiastic, and honest in love, but tend to put your own needs before those of your partner. You are always willing to take the initiative in love and, indeed, thrive on the challenge of a partner who is hard to win. You hate sloppy emotionalism and sentimentality, and always call a spade a spade. No prolonged preliminaries for you. "Desire now, have now" is your motto. But deep down you are a lot less confident than you appear, so you need a partner whose faithfulness you can rely on.

aries' compatibility

Aries–Aries

+ Enjoy each other's go-getting, active attitude to life.
− Accuse each other of selfishness.

Aries–Taurus

+ Aries appreciates Taurus's stability, and Taurus enjoys Aries' liveliness.
− An irresistible force (Aries) meets an immovable object (Taurus).

Aries–Gemini

+ Aries loves Gemini's mind, Gemini enjoys Aries' easy extroversion and friendliness.
− Aries is made insecure by Gemini's elusiveness, Gemini resents Aries' dominating bossiness.

Aries–Cancer

+ Aries enjoys being looked after by Cancer, and Cancer enjoys Aries' dependency.
− Aries feels suffocated by Cancer's emotionality, Cancer feels assaulted by Aries' loudness.

Aries–Leo

+ Aries enjoys Leo's loyalty, Leo enjoys Aries' lively child-likeness.
− They compete with each other to be the center of attention.

Aries–Virgo

+ Aries enjoys the servicing of his or her needs by Virgo, Virgo feels enlivened by Aries.
− Aries thinks Virgo stuffily boring, Virgo is offended by Aries' bossy loudness.

Aries–Libra

+ Great sexual attraction (if of opposite sexes) and enjoy each other's go-gettingness.
− Tend to dislike each other (if of same sex) and there is conflict over who is boss.

Aries–Scorpio

+ Enjoy each other's intensity.
− Aries finds Scorpio sulky and secretive, Scorpio finds Aries shallow.

Aries–Sagittarius

+ Love being "on the go" and traveling together.
− Aries objects to Sagittarius's moralizing attitudes, Sagittarius accuses Aries of irresponsibility.

Aries–Capricorn

+ Aries enjoys the security of Capricorn's sober and responsible attitude to life, Capricorn feels enlivened by Aries.
− Aries accuses Capricorn of being unfeeling, Capricorn accuses Aries of being hysterical.

Aries–Aquarius

+ Aries appreciates Aquarius's independence, Aquarius enjoys Aries' impetuousness.
− Aries is made angry by Aquarius's refusal to be bossed, Aquarius objects to Aries' aggression.

Aries–Pisces

+ Aries enjoys Pisces' willingness to be led, Pisces feels enlivened by Aries.
− Aries is driven crazy by Pisces' passivity, Pisces feels abused by Aries' aggression.

TAURUS

fixed, earth

april 21—may 21

Talents and gifts
Sensuality, wholesomeness, practicality, stability.

Obstacles and challenges
Stubbornness, possessiveness, ultra-conservatism, greed.

You are practical, deep-thinking, organized, and persistent. You love all the good things in life—food, sex, comfortable armchairs, and a tidy bank balance—and you appreciate the delights of all five senses.

On the other hand, you can be stubborn and narrow-minded in your conservatism, like immediately condemning somebody with a tongue-stud, irrespective of any other qualities he or she may have. Physically you are hard-working and strong, but can sometimes be lazy and self-indulgent.

In love, you are affectionate, loyal, lusty, and very possessive. The best things in life may be free, but you are very aware of how expensive the second-best things in life are, so you are inclined to reject a romantic but starving poet in favor of a not-so-romantic businessman (and his credit cards) who can keep you in the manner to which you have become accustomed. Sex, for you, epitomizes all that makes life worth living, but remember the missionary position is not the only way of making love.

taurus's compatibility

Taurus–Aries
+ Aries appreciates Taurus's stability, and Taurus enjoys Aries' liveliness.
− An irresistible force (Aries) meets an immovable object (Taurus).

Taurus–Taurus
+ Appreciate each other's wholesome, stable, sensual attitude to life.
− Accuse each other of stubbornness.

Taurus–Gemini
+ Taurus feels enlivened by Gemini, Gemini feels safe with Taurus.
− Taurus is made insecure by Gemini's flightiness, Gemini feels stifled by Taurus' possessiveness.

Taurus–Cancer
+ They share the aims of enjoying the good things of life and feeling materially and emotionally secure.
− Taurus finds Cancer neurotically unstable, Cancer finds Taurus stolid and emotionally insensitive.

Taurus–Leo
+ Taurus enjoys Leo's romantic nature and generosity, Leo appreciates Taurus's steadfastness and loyalty.
− Mutual accusations of stubborn inflexibility.

Taurus–Virgo
+ Respect each other's shyness, and enjoy each other's quiet sensuality.
− Taurus objects to Virgo's fussiness, Virgo objects to Taurus's unchangingness.

Taurus–Libra
+ Share a love of beauty and order in their surroundings.
− Taurus dislikes Libra's bossiness, Libra dislikes Taurus's stolidness.

Taurus–Scorpio
+ Great sexual attraction (if of opposite sexes), enjoy each other's quiet depth.
− Tend to dislike each other (if of same sex), Taurus dislikes Scorpio's secretiveness, Scorpio dislikes Taurus's bluntness.

Taurus–Sagittarius
+ Taurus feels enlivened by Sagittarius, Sagittarius enjoys Taurus's stability.
− Taurus dislikes Sagittarius's restlessness, Sagittarius feels stifled by Taurus's practicality.

Taurus–Capricorn
+ Taurus values Capricorn's ambition and seriousness, Capricorn enjoys Taurus's conservative values.
− Taurus finds Capricorn mean, Capricorn finds Taurus extravagant.

Taurus–Aquarius
+ Taurus admires Aquarius's independence, Aquarius appreciates Taurus's quiet stability.
− Taurus accuses Aquarius of being cold, Aquarius feels his or her mind intruded by Taurus.

Taurus–Pisces
+ Taurus is appreciative of Pisces' softness and emotional sensitivity, Pisces enjoys Taurus's warm sensuality.
− Taurus dislikes Pisces' elusiveness, Pisces dislikes Taurus's nagging.

GEMINI

mutable, air

may 21–june 20

Talents and gifts
Alertness, curiosity, wit, sociability.

Obstacles and challenges
Superficiality, lack of commitment, fickleness, restlessness.

You are interested in anything and everything, and flit happily between any number of projects you have on the go.

You are talkative, inquisitive, adaptable, responsive, and versatile, but can also easily slip into sarcasm and cruel insensitivity to other people's feelings, justified in the name of wit. You tend to be lithe, energetic, and well-coordinated, but can also be restless, agitated, and nervous. You sing for your supper but need to keep your foot out of your mouth.

In love, companionship is ultimately more important to you than sex. You are playful, flirtatious, and wonderfully entertaining, but you are allergic to commitment and run a mile when the talk turns to love. You can't stand clinging vines, and seek a partner who is a very intelligent friend. But deep down you crave somebody who has the maturity and power to pin you down into stable contentment even though the defiant baby in you is unlikely ever to admit it.

gemini's compatibility

Gemini–Aries

+ Aries loves Gemini's mind, Gemini enjoys Aries' easy extroversion and friendliness.
− Aries is made insecure by Gemini's elusiveness, Gemini resents Aries' dominating bossiness.

Gemini–Taurus

+ Taurus feels enlivened by Gemini, Gemini feels safe with Taurus.
− Taurus is made insecure by Gemini's flightiness, Gemini feels stifled by Taurus's possessiveness.

Gemini–Gemini

+ Enjoy each others' intelligence and talking to each other.
− Mutual accusations of uncaring irresponsibility.

Gemini–Cancer

+ Gemini enjoys being looked after by Cancer, Cancer enjoys Gemini's child-like dependence.
− Gemini feels smothered by Cancer, Cancer feels abused by Gemini's emotional insensitivity.

Gemini–Leo

+ Gemini appreciates Leo's warmth and generosity, Leo enjoys Gemini's lively extroversion.
− Gemini feels Leo is too demanding, Leo feels Gemini is too restless and flighty.

Gemini–Virgo

+ Appreciate each other's minds.
− Gemini objects to Virgo's nit-picking, Virgo accuses Gemini of being facile and shallow.

Gemini–Libra

+ Both enjoy exchanging ideas and talking and laughing together.
− Gemini dislikes Libra's bossiness, Libra dislikes Gemini's lack of commitment.

Gemini–Scorpio

+ Gemini appreciates Scorpio's stable reliability, Scorpio appreciates Gemini's liveliness.
− Gemini feels threatened by Scorpio's reserve, Scorpio feels misunderstood by Gemini's insistence on talking about everything.

Gemini–Sagittarius

+ Great sexual attraction (if of opposite sexes), enjoy exchanging ideas and traveling together.
− Tend to dislike each other (if of same sex), Gemini finds Sagittarius self-righteous, Sagittarius finds Gemini irresponsible.

Gemini–Capricorn

+ Gemini feels safe and secure with Capricorn, Capricorn feels enlivened by Gemini.
− Gemini objects to Capricorn's criticism and stuffiness, Capricorn objects to Gemini's childishness.

Gemini–Aquarius

+ Gemini admires Aquarius's independence, Aquarius enjoys Gemini's intellectual liveliness.
− Gemini feels criticized by Aquarius, Aquarius objects to Gemini's childishness.

Gemini–Pisces

+ Appreciate each other's tolerance of the other's need for privacy.
− Gemini feels smothered by Pisces' emotionality, Pisces feels abused by Gemini's emotional detachment.

CANCER

cardinal, water

june 22–july 22

Talents and gifts
Sympathy, homemaking, motherhood, tenacity.

Obstacles and challenges
Hyper-sensitivity, worrying, infantile demandingness, moodiness.

You are intuitive, perceptive, sympathetic, loyally affectionate, and devotedly committed to your family and home life.

You can be a wonderfully nurturing parent but also a hysterically screaming infant if you are frustrated by others in your desire for their indulgences. You are the keeper of the family heirlooms and photographs and you love remembering and talking about the past. You are excruciatingly aware of the pain in life and a wonderful support to others who are suffering; but you find it difficult to share others' optimism and joy.

In love, you are probably the most romantic of all the signs, full of dreamy tenderness and poetic expressions of your devotion. But you are deeply insecure and needy, and super-sensitive to any slights from others, so you seek a partner who is willing to give you constant reassurance that you are loved unconditionally and eternally. In return, you cook wonderful meals and your lover can count on your commitment through thick and thin.

cancer's compatibility

Cancer–Aries
+ Aries enjoys being looked after by Cancer, and Cancer enjoys Aries' dependency.
− Aries feels suffocated by Cancer's emotionality, Cancer feels assaulted by Aries' loudness.

Cancer–Taurus
+ They share the aims of enjoying the good things of life and feeling materially and emotionally secure.
− Taurus finds Cancer neurotically unstable, Cancer finds Taurus stolid and emotionally insensitive.

Cancer–Gemini
+ Gemini enjoys being looked after by Cancer, Cancer enjoys Gemini's child-like dependence.
− Gemini feels smothered by Cancer, Cancer feels abused by Gemini's emotional insensitivity.

Cancer–Cancer
+ Feel very looked after by each other.
− Conflict about who needs looking after most, and each accuses the other of being too demanding.

Cancer–Leo
+ Cancer basks in Leo's warmth and generosity, Leo feels valued by Cancer's neediness.
− Cancer feels insecure in response to Leo's gregariousness, Leo finds Cancer too clinging.

Cancer–Virgo
+ Cancer enjoys being looked after by Virgo, Virgo enjoys Cancer's neediness.
− Cancer feels criticized by Virgo, Virgo feels unappreciated by Cancer.

Cancer–Libra
+ Cancer admires Libra's independence, Libra appreciates Cancer's sensitivity.
− Cancer feels abused by Libra's forthrightness, Libra feels smothered by Cancer's clinginess.

Cancer–Scorpio
+ Identify with each other's intense emotionality.
− Cancer feels insecure in response to Scorpio's self-sufficiency, Scorpio feels overwhelmed by Cancer's demandingness.

Cancer–Sagittarius
+ Cancer admires and enjoys Sagittarius's easy sociability, Sagittarius admires Cancer's caring nature.
− Cancer is hurt by Sagittarius's bluntness, Sagittarius is upset by Cancer's extreme sensitivity.

Cancer–Capricorn
+ Great sexual attraction (if of opposite sexes), identify with each other's needs for emotional and material security.
− Tend to dislike each other (if of same sex), Cancer accuses Capricorn of being coldly controlling, Capricorn accuses Cancer of being demanding.

Cancer–Aquarius
+ Cancer admires Aquarius's emotional independence, Aquarius respects Cancer's sensitivity.
− Cancer feels inferior to Aquarius, Aquarius feels stifled by Cancer's neediness.

Cancer–Pisces
+ Cancer feels safe with Pisces, Pisces is gratified by Cancer's neediness of him or her.
− Cancer feels unresponded to by Pisces, Pisces feels nagged at and criticized by Cancer.

LEO

fixed, fire

july 23–august 23

Talents and gifts
Warmth, generosity,
loyalty, playfulness.

Obstacles and challenges
Boastfulness, extravagance,
pride, ostentation.

You are organized, confident, inspired, generous, charming, stylish, self-centered, vain, bossy, and cocky. You are proud of your decisiveness and quickness to act on your decisions.

Your warmth and enthusiasm light up any social occasion, and you stand out in a crowd by your bold and flamboyantly colorful clothes. You love luxury, abundance, and high-living in the celebrity classes. If you have it, you flaunt it; if not, you buy it on credit. Eat, drink, and be merry, for tomorrow we die. For better or for worse, you create an immediate impression on others. You, yourself, are also easily impressed, especially by the trappings of status or wealth, which can lead you into making superficial and often false judgements.

In love, you are magnificent, showering your beloved with praise, adoration, romantic surprises, and lavish gifts. You are also a faithful lover unless your pride or vanity is wounded. Woe betide anybody who mocks you or fails to appreciate you.

leo's compatibility

Aries–Leo

+ Aries enjoys Leo's loyalty; Leo enjoys Aries' lively childlike nature.
- They compete with eachother to be the center of attention.

Taurus–Leo

+ Taurus enjoys Leo's romantic nature and generosity; Leo appreciates Taurus's steadfastness and loyalty.
- Mutual accusations of stubborn inflexibility.

Gemini–Leo

+ Gemini appreciates Leo's warmth and generosity; Leo enjoys Gemini's lively extroversion.
- Gemini accuses Leo of being too demanding, Leo accuses Gemini of being too flighty.

Cancer–Leo

+ Cancer basks in Leo's warmth and generosity; Leo feels valued by Cancer's neediness.
- Cancer feels insecure in response to Leo's gregariousness, Leo finds Cancer too clingy.

Leo–Leo

+ Appreciate each other's loyalty and enjoy the good things of life together.
- Accuse each other of being vain and proud.

Leo–Virgo

+ Leo appreciates Virgo's modesty; Virgo enjoys Leo's largesse.
- Leo finds Virgo prissy and lacking in exuberance; Virgo finds Leo vain and extravagant.

Leo–Libra

+ Leo admires Libra's charm and love of beauty; Libra basks in Leo's admiration, and loves him or her wholeheartedly in return.
- Leo objects to Libra's bossiness, Libra objects to Leo's stubbornness.

Leo–Scorpio

+ Leo enjoy Scorpio's passionate sexual responsiveness; Scorpio appreciates Leo's loving faithfulness.
- Leo objects to Scorpio's secretiveness and jealousy. Scorpio objects to Leo's loud extroversion.

Leo–Sagittarius

+ Appreciate each other's easy-going gregariousness and warmth.
- Leo dislikes Sagittarius's restlessness, Sagittarius dislikes Leo's easily hurt vanity and pride.

Leo–Capricorn

+ Leo admires Capricorn's ambition; Capricorn appreciates Leo's taste for the finer things of life.
- Leo finds Capricorn stingy, Capricorn finds Leo extravagant.

Leo–Aquarius

+ Great sexual attraction (if of opposite sexes); Leo admires Aquarius's detachment, Aquarius enjoys Leo's warmth.
- Tend to dislike eachother (if of the same sex). Leo finds Aquarius cold, Aquarius finds Leo boastful and vain.

Leo–Pisces

+ Leo admires Pisces' gentleness; Pisces admires Leo's easy extroversion.
- Leo finds Pisces unappreciative of love and gifts given; Pisces finds Leo arrogant and self-centered.

VIRGO

mutable, earth

august 24–september 23

Talents and gifts
Modesty, helpfulness, discrimination, efficiency.

Obstacles and challenges
Criticality, fussiness, prudishness, shyness.

You are methodical, precise, critical, and worrying. You need routine and order in your life, and you conscientiously look after your health with wholesome food, regular exercise, and enough sleep.

Your shy modesty makes you often overlooked, and you are likely to be the one who, in a social situation, quietly exits from the general hubbub to help your hostess serve supper or do the dishes. Quietly patient, you can happily spend hours alone with your hobbies or even engrossed in untangling a hopelessly knotted ball of string. You love looking after other people but in your fastidiousness, you can become prudishly critical of others' less perfect standards than your own. You need a bit more sloppiness in your life.

In love, you are reticent and shy, but beneath your prim and proper exterior, you are deeply sensual. Once you are assured that you and your lover are both showered and generally thoroughly prepared, you are capable of unbridled orgiastic sensual abandonment. Your quiet, unpretentious faithfulness, conservatism, common sense, practicality, loyalty, and unselfishness are lifelong gifts to your chosen partner.

virgo's compatibility

Virgo–Aries
+ Aries enjoys the servicing of his or her needs by Virgo, Virgo feels enlivened by Aries.
– Aries thinks Virgo stuffily boring, Virgo is offended by Aries' bossy loudness.

Virgo–Taurus
+ Respect each other's shyness, and enjoy each other's quiet sensuality.
– Taurus objects to Virgo's fussiness, Virgo objects to Taurus's unchangingness.

Virgo–Gemini
+ Appreciate each other's minds.
– Gemini objects to Virgo's nit-picking, Virgo accuses Gemini of being facile and shallow.

Virgo–Cancer
+ Cancer enjoys being looked after by Virgo, Virgo enjoys Cancer's neediness.
– Cancer feels criticized by Virgo, Virgo feels unappreciated by Cancer.

Virgo–Leo
+ Leo appreciates Virgo's modesty, Virgo enjoys Leo's largesse.
– Leo finds Virgo prissy and lacking in exuberance, Virgo finds Leo vain and extravagant.

Virgo–Virgo
+ Appreciate each other's quiet self-effacingness.
– Accuse each other of being too critical and perfectionist.

Virgo–Libra
+ Virgo admires Libra's elegance and charm, Libra admires Virgo's modesty.
– Virgo finds Libra bossy and vain, Libra finds Virgo an irritating fuss-pot.

Virgo–Scorpio
+ Appreciate each other's quiet presence.
– Virgo accuses Scorpio of stubbornness, Scorpio accuses Virgo of being too critical.

Virgo–Sagittarius
+ Virgo enjoys looking after Sagittarius, Sagittarius enjoys having his or her physical needs reliably taken care of.
– Virgo finds Sagittarius selfishly demanding, Sagittarius accuses Virgo of being a contining nag.

Virgo–Capricorn
+ Mutual appreciation of each other's quiet sensuality.
– Virgo feels unappreciated by Capricorn, Capricorn feels nagged by Virgo.

Virgo–Aquarius
+ Enjoy rational discussions with each other.
– Virgo feels Aquarius is too emotionally detached, Aquarius feels Virgo is too concerned with petty details.

Virgo–Pisces
+ Great sexual attraction (if of opposite sexes), mutual appreciation of each other's quiet sensitivity and unselfishness.
– Tend to dislike each other (if of the same sex), Virgo finds Pisces impossibly impractical, Pisces finds Virgo unimaginative.

LIBRA

cardinal, air

september 24–october 23

Talents and gifts
Refinement, fairness, charm, tastefulness.

Obstacles and challenges
Insincerity, guile, bossiness, vanity.

You are fair-minded, rational, well-balanced, and kind, but also bossy, vain, manipulative, indecisive, lazy, and procrastinating.

You admire elegance and style in people and things, and ugliness and disorder are deeply distressing to you. You are tactful to a fault because you want to avoid confrontations and quarrels at any cost, but this can lead you into insincerity and manipulativeness towards others, as well as a propensity for your goodwill to be exploited. You need to develop the courage to face the grittier aspects of relationships rather than insisting always on unmitigated pleasantness.

Love is your meaning of life, and relationships of all kinds are infinitely fascinating to you. But "semi-detached" relationships are not for you. You want marriage and lifelong romance as well as intelligent companionship, that's hard to achieve, although you skillfully do your best, creating and maintaining a beautiful home, and adoring and flattering your partner with attention and overindulgence. You want the same in return and are deeply hurt and disappointed if this is not forthcoming.

libra's compatibility

Libra–Aries
+ Great sexual attraction (if of opposite sexes) and enjoy each other's go-gettingness.
– Tend to dislike each other (if of same sex) and there is conflict over who is boss.

Libra–Taurus
+ Share a love of beauty and order in their surroundings.
– Taurus dislikes Libra's bossiness, Libra dislikes Taurus's stolidness.

Libra–Gemini
+ Both enjoy exchanging ideas and talking and laughing together.
– Gemini dislikes Libra's bossiness, Libra dislikes Gemini's lack of commitment.

Libra–Cancer
+ Cancer admires Libra's independence, Libra appreciates Cancer's sensitivity.
– Cancer feels abused by Libra's forthrightness, Libra feels smothered by Cancer's clinginess.

Libra–Leo
+ Leo admires Libra's charm and love of beauty, Libra basks in Leo's admiration, and loves him or her wholeheartedly in return.
– Leo objects to Libra's bossiness, Libra objects to Leo's stubbornness.

Libra–Virgo
+ Virgo admires Libra's elegance and charm, Libra admires Virgo's modesty.
– Virgo finds Libra bossy and vain, Libra finds Virgo an irritating fuss-pot.

Libra–Libra
+ Share a love of beauty and harmony and enjoyment of luxury.
– Compete for dominance.

Libra–Scorpio
+ Libra enjoys Scorpio's passionate sexiness, Scorpio enjoys Libra's erotic artfulness.
– Libra feels unloved by Scorpio's silences, Scorpio feels intruded upon by Libra's insistent talking.

Libra–Sagittarius
+ Enjoy each other's minds and easy-going sociability and optimism.
– Libra finds Sagittarius crude and offensively blunt, Sagittarius finds Libra vain and bossy.

Libra–Capricorn
+ Enjoy each other's sense of humor.
– Libra finds Capricorn a miserable pessimist, Capricorn finds Libra wasteful and vain.

Libra–Aquarius
+ Enjoy each other's friendship and detached interest in the world.
– Libra finds Aquarius coldly arrogant, Aquarius finds Libra self-centered and vain.

Libra–Pisces
+ Appreciate each other's gentleness and liking for peace.
– Libra finds Pisces too passive, Pisces finds Libra too bossy.

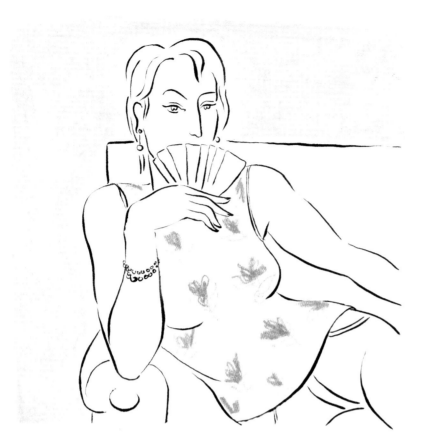

SCORPIO

fixed, water

october 24–november 22

Talents and gifts
Depth, passion, determination, self-mastery.

Obstacles and challenges
Vengefulness, suspiciousness, jealousy, brooding.

You are perceptive, inquisitive, assertive, shrewd, courageous, obsessive, cynical, critical, and vengeful. You love secrets and solving mysteries, and the challenge of making lots of money in business.

You are very suspicious of others' motives and believe you have to defend yourself against being harmed by staying very controlled and not wearing your heart on your sleeve. You are an excellent detective, and Poker is probably your favorite game. You have an aura of mystery and magnetism that fascinates and scares everyone who meets you.

In love, you are passionately committed, intense, and excruciatingly jealous. Sex, for you, is a transcendental, sacred, mystical experience—the ultimate meaning of life in the face of death. Betrayal is unbearable to you, forgiveness is not in your nature, and you will go to extreme lengths to wreak vengeance on a cheating partner. For better or for worse, you are unforgettable—in and out of bed. Being with you is like living a scene out of Othello.

scorpio's compatibility

Scorpio–Aries
+ Enjoy each other's intensity.
– Aries finds Scorpio sulky and secretive, Scorpio finds Aries shallow.

Scorpio–Taurus
+ Great sexual attraction (if of opposite sexes), enjoy each other's quiet depth.
– Tend to dislike each other (if of same sex), Taurus dislikes Scorpio's secretiveness, Scorpio dislikes Taurus's bluntness.

Scorpio–Gemini
+ Gemini appreciates Scorpio's stable reliability, Scorpio appreciates Gemini's liveliness.
– Gemini feels threatened by Scorpio's reserve, Scorpio feels misunderstood by Gemini's insistence on talking about everything.

Scorpio–Cancer
+ Identify with each other's intense emotionality.
– Cancer feels insecure in response to Scorpio's self-sufficiency, Scorpio feels overwhelmed by Cancer's demandingness.

Scorpio–Leo
+ Leo enjoys Scorpio's passionate sexual responsiveness, Scorpio appreciates Leo's loving faithfulness.
– Leo objects to Scorpio's secretiveness and jealousy, Scorpio objects to Leo's loud extroversion.

Scorpio–Virgo
+ Appreciate each other's quiet presence.
– Virgo accuses Scorpio of stubbornness, Scorpio accuses Virgo of being too critical.

Scorpio–Libra
+ Libra enjoys Scorpio's passionate sexiness, Scorpio enjoys Libra's erotic artfulness.
– Libra feels unloved by Scorpio's silences, Scorpio feels intruded upon by Libra's insistent talking.

Scorpio–Scorpio
+ Mutual emotional depth and intensity.
– Accuse each other of possessive jealousy.

Scorpio–Sagittarius
+ Scorpio admires Sagittarius's honesty, Sagittarius is intrigued by Scorpio's self-control.
– Scorpio dislikes Sagittarius's crudeness and social clumsiness, Sagittarius is intimidated by Scorpio's piercing insight.

Scorpio–Capricorn
+ Admire and appreciate each other's serious attitudes to life.
– Scorpio finds Capricorn overly materialistic, Capricorn is suspicious of Scorpio's secretiveness.

Scorpio–Aquarius
+ Enjoy intellectual analysis with each other.
– Mutually accuse each other of obstinacy, Scorpio finds Aquarius too detached, Aquarius finds Scorpio too intense.

Scorpio–Pisces
+ Are at ease with each other's silent presence.
– Scorpio finds Pisces too tolerant, Pisces finds Scorpio too rigid.

SAGITTARIUS

mutable, fire

november 23–december 21

Talents and gifts
Friendliness, enthusiasm, optimism, largesse.

Obstacles and challenges
Crudeness, inconsiderateness, clumsiness, unreliability.

You are friendly, cheerful, broad-minded, optimistic, witty and also blunt, opinionated, intolerant, and grandiose.

Freedom is extremely important to you, so you hate being asked to make committed plans or arrangements. You like to do everything on the spur of the moment. Your bright and breezy sociability makes you popular as a guest despite your unreliability and tactlessness that is clumsy rather than badly intentioned. You want to see life through rose-colored spectacles and can't stand people who are miserably pessimistic.

In love, your intentions are honourable, but you lack diplomacy and finesse in courtship. You tend to be a good-natured big baby who is actually looking for a strong partner to organize and control you, even though you protest that you don't want to be pinned down. You like lusty, straightforward sex mixed with open and honest talk. You can't cope with much subtlety or indirectness, but you love intelligent, speculative conversation and you are never boring.

sagittarius's compatibility

Sagittarius–Aries

+ Love being "on the go" and traveling together.
– Aries objects to Sagittarius's moralizing attitudes, Sagittarius accuses Aries of irresponsibility.

Sagittarius–Taurus

+ Taurus feels enlivened by Sagittarius, Sagittarius enjoys Taurus's stability.
– Taurus dislikes Sagittarius's restlessness, Sagittarius feels stifled by Taurus's practicality.

Sagittarius–Gemini

+ Great sexual attraction (if of opposite sexes), enjoy exchanging ideas and traveling together.
– Tend to dislike each other (if of same sex), Gemini finds Sagittarius self-righteous, Sagittarius finds Gemini irresponsible.

Sagittarius–Cancer

+ Cancer admires and enjoys Sagittarius's easy sociability, Sagittarius admires Cancer's caring nature.
– Cancer is hurt by Sagittarius's bluntness, Sagittarius is upset by Cancer's extreme sensitivity.

Sagittarius–Leo

+ Appreciate each other's easy-going gregariousness and warmth.
– Leo dislikes Sagittarius's restlessness, Sagittarius dislikes Leo's easily hurt vanity and pride.

Sagittarius–Virgo

+ Virgo enjoys looking after Sagittarius, Sagittarius enjoys having his or her physical needs reliably taken care of.
– Virgo finds Sagittarius selfishly demanding, Sagittarius accuses Virgo of being a confining nag.

Sagittarius–Libra

+ Enjoy each other's minds and easy-going sociability and optimism.
– Libra finds Sagittarius crude and offensively blunt, Sagittarius finds Libra vain and bossy.

Sagittarius–Scorpio

+ Scorpio admires Sagittarius's honesty, Sagittarius is intrigued by Scorpio's self-control.
– Scorpio dislikes Sagittarius's crudeness and social clumsiness, Sagittarius is intimidated by Scorpio's piercing insight.

Sagittarius–Sagittarius

+ Enjoy each other's boisterous good nature.
– Accuse each other of selfish inattentiveness to the practicalities of life.

Sagittarius–Capricorn

+ Sagittarius admires Capricorn's self-discipline, Capricorn admires Sagittarius's easy extroversion.
– Sagittarius dislikes Capricorn's dour pessimism, Capricorn feels invaded by Sagittarius's boisterousness.

Sagittarius–Aquarius

+ Enjoy sharing and discussing intellectual ideas with each other.
– Sagittarius finds Aquarius cold, Aquarius dislikes Sagittarius's intrusive bluntness.

Sagittarius–Pisces

+ Sagittarius enjoys and respects Pisces' spirituality, Pisces appreciates Sagittarius's wide-ranging ideas.
– Sagittarius finds Pisces too vague, Pisces finds Sagittarius too blunt.

CAPRICORN

cardinal, earth

december 22–january 20

Talents and gifts

Reliability, conscientiousness, responsibility, industriousness.

Obstacles and challenges

Meanness, pessimism, gloominess, intolerance.

You are deep, practical, methodical, serious, persevering and responsible, and you make an excellent, if stern, boss or leader.

Other people may see you as pessimistic and mean, but experience has taught you that life is not a bed of roses and self-denial and hard work are the price of success. You are ambitious for status, and a secure future and a comfortable old-age, rather than for the pleasures of today, and you can be resentful and bitter towards people who seem to achieve wealth or distinction without effort or self-denial.

In love, you seek a partner who shares your conservative values but who also adds a bit of lightness to your somber nature. In the privacy of the bedroom, you are deeply sensual and a marathon performer, but you rarely display your love for your partner in public. Propriety is your second name. You remember birthdays and anniversaries although the presents you give usually have lasting value rather than being the romantic gestures your partner may sometimes wish for.

capricorn's compatibility

Capricorn–Aries
+ Aries enjoys the security of Capricorn's sober and responsible attitude to life, Capricorn feels enlivened by Aries.
− Aries accuses Capricorn of being unfeeling, Capricorn accuses Aries of being hysterical.

Capricorn–Taurus
+ Taurus values Capricorn's ambition and seriousness, Capricorn enjoys Taurus's conservative values.
− Taurus finds Capricorn mean, Capricorn finds Taurus extravagant.

Capricorn–Gemini
+ Gemini feels safe and secure with Capricorn, Capricorn feels enlivened by Gemini.
− Gemini objects to Capricorn's criticism and stuffiness, Capricorn objects to Gemini's childishness.

Capricorn–Cancer
+ Great sexual attraction (if of opposite sexes), identify with each other's needs for emotional and material security.
− Tend to dislike each other (if of same sex), Cancer accuses Capricorn of being coldly controlling, Capricorn accuses Cancer of being demanding.

Capricorn–Leo
+ Leo admires Capricorn's ambition, Capricorn appreciates Leo's liking for the finer things of life.
− Leo finds Capricorn mean, Capricorn finds Leo extravagant.

Capricorn–Virgo
+ Mutual appreciation of each other's quiet sensuality.
− Virgo feels unappreciated by Capricorn, Capricorn feels nagged by Virgo.

Capricorn–Libra
+ Enjoy each other's sense of humor.
− Libra finds Capricorn a miserable pessimist, Capricorn finds Libra wasteful and vain.

Capricorn–Scorpio
+ Admire and appreciate each other's serious attitudes to life.
− Scorpio finds Capricorn overly materialistic, Capricorn is suspicious of Scorpio's secretiveness.

Capricorn–Sagittarius
+ Sagittarius admires Capricorn's self-discipline, Capricorn admires Sagittarius's easy extroversion.
− Sagittarius dislikes Capricorn's dour pessimism, Capricorn feels invaded by Sagittarius's boisterousness.

Capricorn–Capricorn
+ Appreciate each other's serious, self disciplined approach to life and desire for achievement.
− Feel personally neglected by each other's concentration on worldly ambitions.

Capricorn–Aquarius
+ Appreciate each other's seriousness and detachment.
− Capricorn finds Aquarius too idealistic, Aquarius finds Capricorn too materialistic.

Capricorn–Pisces
+ Capricorn admires Pisces' spirituality, Pisces admires Capricorn's self-motivation.
− Capricorn dislikes Pisces' passivity, Pisces dislikes Capricorn's materialism.

AQUARIUS

fixed, air

january 21–february 19

Talents and gifts
Independence, originality, political idealism, friendship.

Obstacles and challenges
Dogmatism, detachedness, aloofness, lack of sympathy.

You are inquisitive, witty and original, independent, self-sufficient, and whacky, as well as argumentative, intolerant, bossy, and emotionally distant.

You pride yourself on your highly idealistic principles although you apply these more to humanity at large rather than to intimate others. Your friends and colleagues are very important to you, and you are very loyal to them, but you are not a touchy-feely kind of person and you shy away from gushy, sentimental people.

In love, you are a bit of a cynic and are pragmatically ready to settle for what is available. In fact, you tend to be a bit of a do-gooder in your relationships and are often drawn to partners with glaring faults, with the intention of reforming them. You rarely succeed in this aim but realistically accept that marriages are not made in heaven. What is lacking in your love life you make up for through your career and other friendships.

aquarius's compatibility

Aquarius–Aries
+ Aries appreciates Aquarius's independence, Aquarius enjoys Aries' impetuousness.
− Aries is made angry by Aquarius's refusal to be bossed, Aquarius objects to Aries' aggression.

Aquarius–Taurus
+ Taurus admires Aquarius's independence, Aquarius appreciates Taurus's quiet stability.
− Taurus accuses Aquarius of being cold, Aquarius feels his or her mind intruded by Taurus.

Aquarius–Gemini
+ Gemini admires Aquarius's independence, Aquarius enjoys Gemini's intellectual liveliness.
− Gemini feels criticized by Aquarius, Aquarius objects to Gemini's childishness.

Aquarius–Cancer
+ Cancer admires Aquarius's emotional independence, Aquarius respects Cancer's sensitivity.
− Cancer feels inferior to Aquarius, Aquarius feels stifled by Cancer's neediness.

Aquarius–Leo
+ Great sexual attraction (if of opposite sexes), Leo admires Aquarius's detachment, Aquarius enjoys Leo's warmth.
− Tend to dislike each other (if of the same sex), Leo finds Aquarius cold, Aquarius finds Leo boastful and vain.

Aquarius–Virgo
+ Enjoy rational discussions with each other.
− Virgo feels Aquarius is too emotionally detached, Aquarius feels Virgo is too concerned with petty details.

Aquarius–Libra
+ Enjoy each other's friendship and detached interest in the world.
− Libra finds Aquarius coldly arrogant, Aquarius finds Libra self-centered and vain.

Aquarius–Scorpio
+ Enjoy intellectual analysis with each other.
− Mutually accuse each other of obstinacy, Scorpio finds Aquarius too detached, Aquarius finds Scorpio too intense.

Aquarius–Sagittarius
+ Enjoy sharing and discussing intellectual ideas with each other.
− Sagittarius finds Aquarius cold, Aquarius dislikes Sagittarius's intrusive bluntness.

Aquarius–Capricorn
+ Appreciate each other's seriousness and detachment.
− Capricorn finds Aquarius too idealistic, Aquarius finds Capricorn too materialistic.

Aquarius–Aquarius
+ Enjoy each other's intelligent, detached observations.
− Accuse each other of obstinate inflexibility.

Aquarius–Pisces
+ Aquarius admires Pisces' spirituality, Pisces admires Aquarius's intellectuality.
− Aquarius finds Pisces too emotional and passive, Pisces feels rejected by Aquarius's independence.

PISCES

mutable, water

february 20—march 20

Talents and gifts
Compassion, imagination, gentleness, kindness.

Obstacles and challenges
Passivity, vagueness, indecisiveness, self-effacement.

You are intuitive, imaginative, gentle, compassionate, solitary, nervous, fearful, vague, and confused.

While others may see you as an escapist, from your point of view the push and shove of the rat race holds no appeal and you look forward to the earliest possible retirement when you can spend your time enjoying simple sensual pleasures and dreaming. You are not much of a talker but people often judge you a good conversationalist because you patiently listen to them unburden themselves of all their woes.

In love, you seek a deeply wounded other on whom you can pour all your compassionate, healing devotion. You also need a partner with some rambunctiousness and spunkiness to intrude on your dreamy solitude and make you feel fully alive. Sexually, you are tender and gentle rather than lusty, and you seem to want nothing more than to please your partner. But there are times when your self-abnegation turns into sadistic passive-aggression that causes your partner considerable frustration and grief.

pisces' compatibility

Pisces–Aries

+ Aries enjoys Pisces' willingness to be led, Pisces feels enlivened by Aries.

− Aries is driven crazy by Pisces' passivity, Pisces feels abused by Aries' aggression.

Pisces–Taurus

+ Taurus is appreciative of Pisces' softness and emotional sensitivity, Pisces enjoys Taurus's warm sensuality.

− Taurus dislikes Pisces' elusiveness, Pisces dislikes Taurus's nagging.

Pisces–Gemini

+ Appreciate each other's tolerance of the other's need for privacy.

− Gemini feels smothered by Pisces emotionality, Pisces feels abused by Gemini's emotional detachment.

Pisces–Cancer

+ Cancer feels safe with Pisces, Pisces is gratified by Cancer's neediness of him or her.

− Cancer feels unresponded to by Pisces, Pisces feels nagged and criticized by Cancer.

Pisces–Leo

+ Leo admires Pisces' gentleness, Pisces admires Leo's easy extroversion.

− Leo finds Pisces unappreciative of love and gifts given, Pisces finds Leo arrogant and self-centered.

Pisces–Virgo

+ Great sexual attraction (if of opposite sexes), mutual appreciation of each other's quiet sensitivity and unselfishness.

− Tend to dislike each other (if of the same sex), Virgo finds Pisces impossibly impractical, Pisces finds Virgo unimaginative.

Pisces–Libra

+ Appreciate each other's gentleness and liking for peace.

− Libra finds Pisces too passive, Pisces finds Libra too bossy.

Pisces–Scorpio

+ Are at ease with each other's silent presence.

− Scorpio finds Pisces too tolerant, Pisces finds Scorpio too rigid.

Pisces–Sagittarius

+ Sagittarius enjoys and respects Pisces' spirituality, Pisces appreciates Sagittarius's wide-ranging ideas.

− Sagittarius finds Pisces too vague, Pisces finds Sagittarius too blunt.

Pisces–Capricorn

+ Capricorn admires Pisces' spirituality, Pisces admires Capricorn's self-motivation.

− Capricorn dislikes Pisces' passivity, Pisces dislikes Capricorn's materialism.

Pisces–Aquarius

+ Aquarius admires Pisces' spirituality, Pisces admires Aquarius's intellectuality.

− Aquarius finds Pisces too emotional and passive, Pisces feels rejected by Aquarius's independence.

Pisces–Pisces

+ Share a compassionate sensitivity to each other's and the world's suffering.

− Accuse each other of being confused and unrealistic.

the transits of life

Astrology has more to teach us about ourselves than is given in our birth horoscope. Over the passage of our lives, the slow-moving outer planets (Jupiter, Saturn, Chiron, Uranus, Neptune, and Pluto) move into significant positions (transits) in the heavens when compared to their locations in our birth horoscopes. Each type of position (called a configuration) signals a new stage of life. The configurations they form are called the conjunction, the sextile, the trine, the square, and the opposition, and they all have different stories to tell.

These life indicators are not dependent on your birth date, but on your age. So, whatever year you are born in, when you reach 63 years of age, you have Saturn square Saturn. We are all aware that different age groups have different interests and preoccupations. What you may not be aware of is that these tendencies are a reflection of what is in the heavens. By recognizing through astrology where you are on life's journey, you can learn more about yourself and your relationships. The following are brief descriptions of all the important universally experienced transits of adult life, and how they are likely to affect your love life.

if you are 17–19 years old: you have Jupiter opposition Jupiter and Saturn trine Saturn

These transits declare that the worst is over concerning the turbulence of adolescence. You now probably get on better with your parents than you have done for years and you are feeling exuberantly enthusiastic about life and justly proud of

the planets and configurations

As each transiting planet configures its own position in your natal horoscope, it has a particular influence on your life.

Jupiter: expansion and optimism are generally the order of the day.

Saturn: there is important learning to do, whether we like it or not, in the interest of becoming more mature.

Chiron: circumstances force us to face issues we would rather avoid, but we will be rewarded with a great sense of relief.

Uranus: life becomes excitingly—even nerve-rackingly—unpredictable.

Neptune: we often feel confused and uncertain; we also have an increased appreciation of music, poetry, and all imaginative experiences in life.

Pluto: we are called on to dredge up unfinished business from the past and deal with it once and for all.

All the outer planet transits are somewhat modified by the different kinds of configurations they form.

The conjunction: there are important and inevitable new beginnings.

The sextile: opportunities are offered to us.

The trine: these are times of ease and pleasure.

The square: inner conflicts need to be resolved.

The opposition: challenging circumstances outside our control have to be faced.

your educational achievements. You are preparing calmly and with self-discipline, looking forward to further education or happily beginning your first real job and the acceptance of adult responsibilities. You may also be embarking on your first serious sexual relationship.

if you are 21–22 years old: you have Saturn square Saturn and Uranus square Uranus

You are now stepping out into the grown up world in earnest and are aware that you have to make some important choices. Should you sow your wild oats, travel around the world and generally live for today, or settle down into a long-term relationship and establish a career? While you may manage to do a bit of both, by and large you are likely to choose either the path of freedom or the path of constraint. Perhaps for the first time you realize that every choice we make involves giving up something else.

if you are 22–25 years old: you have Jupiter conjunction Jupiter and Saturn sextile Saturn

Generally, your life is going very well. Whatever path you have chosen, you are now pursuing with enthusiasm and appropriate self-discipline. You feel fully part of the adult world and, if you have not already done so, this is the time when you feel the need to fully leave your parents and set up a home of your own. But you will still value your parents' support and probably enjoy visiting them regularly. Your love life is likely to be stable and contented.

if you are 28–30 years old: you have Saturn conjunction Saturn, Uranus trine Uranus, and Neptune sextile Neptune

This is a time of reckoning and one of the most significant turning points in your life. You may have felt grown-up before, but this is the beginning of true adulthood when you discover the harsh reality that the world is not your oyster, but rather that your life is severely circumscribed by your abilities, your childhood conditioning, and the consequences of the choices you have already made. Depression is common at this time, accompanied by a feeling of "my life is nearly half over and I've achieved nothing!" In truth, the life of your autonomous self is just beginning. If you rebelled against staid conventionality at 21, you probably now feel the urgent desire to settle down; if you chose the responsible path at 21, you may feel you have locked yourself into a prison from which you now desperately want to escape. Relationships and careers are going through a severe testing time and are likely to be abandoned if they are no longer suited to the person you have become. Childhood is over, and your true adulthood begins now with the realization that only you can make your dreams come true by what you are willing to do for yourself.

if you are 34 years old: you have Saturn sextile Saturn

As when you were 24–25, this is a time of equilibrium and balance in your life. You are pursuing your career goals and may have happily started a family of your own.

if you are 35–36 years old: you have Saturn square Saturn

Although you have been pursuing your chosen path sensibly and progressively for the past few years, you now feel a bit depressed. You have eaten the icing off your cake and the cake is beginning to taste a bit stale. Your ambitions may be well on the way to fulfillment, but one way or another, life seems full of duty and responsibility, and you are inclined to feel, "Is this all?" In your love life you may well be feeling a seven-year-itch.

redressing the balance

★ What were the feelings of optimism you had when you were 17–19 years old?
★ Did you choose freedom or security when you were 21–22 years old?
★ What did you learn from the route you took?
★ What did you give up?
★ How did you redress the balance of this choice at 28–30?

if you are 38–44 years old: you have Saturn opposition Saturn, Uranus opposition Uranus, Neptune square Neptune, and Pluto square Pluto

Now changes and uncertainties crowd in on one another and you may wonder if you will ever again be free of depression, self-doubt, onerous burdens and obligations, nervous instability, confusion about anything and everything, painful confrontations, and having to deal with your deepest hang-ups. You are aware now of the consequences of choices you made about 14 years ago, and the goals you set yourself then may now seem illusory in terms of the satisfactions you expected.

In contrast, at the same time, you feel excited because this is also a time of revelation, when your mind is opened to new possibilities that you have never before even dreamt of. If you think back now to your previous Saturn opposition when you were just 14 or 15 years old, you may remember some ambitions and dreams of glory that you had then that you long ago forgot about. Now is the time to bring them to the surface again and perhaps seek their fulfillment. At first, in response to the excitement of this time, you may become defiant in whatever area of life is central to your new awareness. However, gradually, over the course of your forties, you will come to recognize the old and the new as two sides of one coin, both of which have validity in your life.

Obviously, your love life is likely to be tested in these years and you are likely to abandon relationships that have outlived their purpose for you. A good relationship will survive the challenges of this time, even though you and your partner will probably find it necessary to reassess what you want from each other.

changes and uncertainties

★ What hang-ups did you face between 38 and 44?

★ What revelations did you have?

★ What new experiences or growth in consciousness were associated with those revelations?

★ Did you rekindle any ambitions or dreams?

★ How was your love life tested during this time?

★ Where did you find renewed satisfaction and security at 47?

if you are 47 years old: you have Saturn trine Saturn

Now you are working steadily and responsibly within the established structures of your life, which gives you a feeling of general satisfaction and a sense of security.

if you are 49–51 years old: you have Saturn square Saturn and Chiron conjunction Chiron

You will have experienced several previous significant Chiron transits to its position in your natal horoscope but, because Chiron's orbit is very erratic, these transits will have occurred at a variety of ages for different individuals. But, for everybody, Chiron forms a conjunction to its natal position at age 51.

You have no option now but to admit that you are middle-aged and you are likely to feel a last urgent sense of ambitious energy "before it is too late." You may also feel that—at last—you have properly healed any deep wounds left over from your childhood, with a consequent dissolution of fears you have lived with up until now. You are beginning to experience some serene self-acceptance.

For women, this is the time of the menopause, and even though you may have long ago completed your family, it is difficult to avoid a sense of poignancy that you can no longer have any more children. You may, however, be beginning to look forward to grandchildren.

If your relationship with your partner is essentially good, you will together make plans for a new era of relative freedom in your lives, probably with more money and fewer responsibilities than you have had for a very long time. But if you have kept a relationship going for more practical considerations, you may break up now and seek a new lover for the new you.

if you are 54 years old: you have Saturn sextile Saturn

The challenges that you met between 49 and 51 are now established new structures in your life and you have opportunities for satisfying work associated with those structures. If this is the time when the last of your children is leaving home and you have delayed a radical reassessment of your life until now, now you will do it. If an unsatisfactory relationship has passed its sell-by date, now you will discard it.

if you are 56–60 years old: you have Saturn conjunction Saturn, Uranus trine Uranus, and Neptune trine Neptune

This time is in many ways a recapitulation of the "identity crisis" you experienced between 28 and 30. You are again forced to face your limitations and again feel that "time is running out". 28–30 brought you awareness of the limitations that your abilities and your childhood conditioning imposed on you in the pursuit of your ambitions; 56–60 brings you awareness of how far you have fulfilled your ambitions, and a recognition that your achievement in the wider world is essentially over. Now you want more time to enjoy contemplative pursuits, general relaxation, and the enjoyment of life for its own sake.

While you may not be able to gain much more power in the external world, this is compensated for by your realization that you now care more for self-approval than for the world's evaluation of you. In your love life, you may be facing the challenge of your own and your partner's retirement from work and the need to make appropriate adjustments associated with being together much more than you had to previously.

if you are 63 years old: you have Saturn square Saturn and Uranus square Uranus

You last had these transits when you were 21–22. Now, as then, you are required to find a balance between freedom and structure in your life. Old age is on the horizon and, if you have not already done so, you will soon retire. You need to discover some new and absorbing activities for your retirement years.
Your love life will now be either contented and serene or else you will make a last-ditch bid for freedom from a relationship that is stale and lifeless.

a new era

- ★ How did you expend your ambition energy between 49 and 51?
- ★ What fears were finally laid to rest?
- ★ What new era of your life did you embark on in your 50s?
- ★ What limitations and achievements did you recognize between 56 and 60?
- ★ Have you expanded your spiritual orientation to life and found increased serenity since your 60s?

if you are 70 years old: you have Saturn opposition Saturn and Uranus sextile Uranus

You last had these transits when you were 14–15 years old, and you first became aware of the limitations imposed on you by external reality. You were also excitedly looking forward to new freedom. Now you are aware of the limitations imposed on you by your natural life-span and you need to come to terms with the inevitability of death. But at the same time you have a sense that your duties are finished and, with whatever life is left to you, you are entitled to "do your own thing." If you are widowed or divorced, you may surprise your children (and grandchildren) by falling in love again and behaving like a frisky adolescent!

if you are 84–88 years old: you have Saturn conjunction Saturn, Uranus conjunction Uranus, and Neptune opposition Neptune

Now you can survey the whole of your life with wisdom and detachment. Ideally, you can withdraw from the mundane concerns of the world in favor of a serene, mystical transcendence of your self and all its fears and strivings. You feel benign love for all humankind.

step three
do it now

By the time our first Saturn cycle is complete, when we are 28–30 years old, most of us realize that there are no free lunches in life: we get what we pay for. The matter of love is no exception and, despite our eternal quest for true romance, the game of love is as fraught with a vulnerability and pain as it is with joy.

It is through the pain as well as the joy of loving that we achieve most of our personal growth. We cannot avoid pain, but we can mitigate it greatly by an awareness that we and our lovers are equals in our human frailty. Our horoscopes are like hands of cards we have been dealt and it behoves us to be aware that our lovers' hands are different but equal in value to our own. Sort your cards and ascertain the strengths and weaknesses of your own and your partner's hands. Play cooperatively, attentively, and with finesse and pleasure.

make the best of the stars

Now you've read through these pages, look inwards at the jigsaw puzzle of your life. In your Sun sign, recognize your positive and negative aspects, and be glad for both. In your life cycles, see if you can identify the choices you have faced, and decisions you have made—and see what lies ahead for you. If you have not yet experienced the stage of questioning and decision-making that comes at 38–44 years of age, the whole picture is probably unclear, but beyond that point you can probably see what the completed picture is going to be, even though it is not yet complete. Ask yourself the following questions:

★ Are you making the most of your present stage of development?
★ What do you anticipate you will do at the next significant challenging stage in your life?

If you want to be happy, be.

Leo Tolstoy (1828–1910)

Now you've come to the end of your programme, it's time to take stock of where you are and how far you've come. It's been quite a journey, hasn't it? You've taken the first steps on the quest for happiness and, once started, there's no stopping you. If you haven't found your true love yet, you will. He is out there just waiting for you to come along, so that you can make each other's happiness complete.

You may like to write a list of the most important things you have learned about yourself, your attitude to happiness and love and your relationships. Keep this in your journal and look back at it from time to time.

Every day, continue doing any affirmations you've found especially important. Try to live in the present. Don't live in the future or the past—neither of those places is real. Whenever you find yourself worrying, pull yourself back to the now.

Treat yourself once a week to an hour of quiet meditation to clear your mind. Then spend some time simply examining yourself and your life and how you're feeling. Listening to your own inner voice is the most powerful thing you can do to enrich your life.

We hope you will come back to this book—and to your own journal—whenever you feel in need of a bit of advice or comfort. Treat it as a rainy-day book. On your on-going life journey, try to remember that none of us is happy all the time. You need the lows to appreciate the highs. But it is possible to feel pretty good most of the time, and when you're feeling down, you now know how to take steps to make yourself feel better.

When you feel good, the people around you feel good too, so a little happiness sends ripples out into the wider community. By taking care of your own happiness, you are benefiting everyone.

Go well … and live happily ever after.

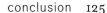

index

a

action, circle of, 43
affirmations, 27
Air, Sun signs, 88, 89
Aquarius, 112–13
Aries, 92–3
assertiveness, 80–2
astrology, 85–123
attentiveness, 78

b

bad habits, 30–1
beliefs, 32–6
blame, removing, 81
body language, 42, 72

c

Cancer, 98–9
Capricorn, 110–11
cardinality, Sun signs, 89
Chiron, astrology, 116–17, 120
circle of action, 43
circle of love, 21
clothes, 56, 71
communication, 48–83
communication styles, 64–9
compatibility, Sun signs, 91, 93–115
confidence, 42, 51–3
conversation, 58–63, 74

e

Earth, Sun signs, 88, 89
elements, Sun signs, 88–9
empathy, 62, 70, 82
enigmatic women, 78
eye contact, 77

f

facial expressions, 72
fears, 24–5
feedback, 57
Fire, Sun signs, 88, 89
first impressions, 50–9
fixity, Sun signs, 89
flirtatiousness, 77
framing experiences, 28
future, beliefs about, 33–6

g

Gemini, 96–7
goals, 38–9

h

habits, changing, 30–1
humor, 78

i

"I love you," ways to say, 82
inner voice, 25
intelligence, sex appeal, 77

j

Jupiter, astrology, 116–18

k

knowing yourself, 14–21

l

learning in progress, 18
Leo, 100–1
Libra, 104–5
listening skills, 60–3
love journals, 13, 19, 45
love-ability, 22

m

matching, building
  rapport, 70–3
mind, states of, 40–1
mirrors, self-observation,
  56
mismatching rapport, 73,
  74
modalities, Sun signs,
  88–9
mood, states of mind,
  40–1
movement, building
  rapport, 72
mutability, Sun signs, 89

n

names, remembering, 59
needs, expressing, 80–2
negative aspects of love,
  20–1
negative thoughts, 26
Neptune, astrology,
  116–19, 121, 122

p

past experiences, 34
personal boundary space,
  43
personality types, 54 6
Pisces, 114–15
planets, transits, 116 22
playfulness, 77
Pluto, astrology, 116–17,
  119
positive aspects of love,
  20–1

positive thinking, 26–7
posture, 42, 72
power, sex appeal, 78
pros and cons of love,
  20–1

r

rapport:
  breaking, 74
  building, 70–3
re-framing, 28
rhythms, building rapport,
  72
romance, sex appeal, 78

s

Sagittarius, 108–9
Saturn, astrology, 116–22,
  123
Scorpio, 106–7
self-esteem, 22
sensuality, 77
sex appeal, 76–9
small talk, 58–9
space, personal, 43
states of mind, 40–1
strengths, knowing
  yourself, 18–19
Sun signs, 88–123
"swish pattern," 30–1

t

talking, 58–9, 72
Taurus, 94–5
transits, planets, 116–22

u

unconscious mind, 27
Uranus, astrology,
  116–19, 121, 122

v

values, 16
Virgo, 102–3

w

Water, Sun signs, 88, 89
weaknesses, knowing
  yourself, 18–19
wheel of life, 15

z

zodiac, 88

further reading

Awaken the Giant Within by Anthony Robbins (1992)

Introducing Neuro-Linguistic Programming
by Joseph O'Connor and John Seymour (1993)

Life Coaching by Eileen Mulligan (1999)

Loving What Is by Katie Byron (2002)

Nonviolent Communication by Marshall B. Rosenberg (2002)

Principles of NLP by Joseph O'Connor and Ian McDermott (1996)

The NLP Coach by Ian McDermott and Wendy Jago (2001)

Unlimited Power by Anthony Robbins (1989)

Words that Change Minds
by Shelle Rose Charvet (1997)